In *Untying Your Knots*, Fritz Ridenour takes a positive, practical approach to loosening the emotional knots that may tie you up, slow you down, and keep you from contentment. He begins with two essentials for untying your knots: trusting God to help you and acting on the belief that He will. Then through biblical insights and intriguing anecdotes, Ridenour provides strong, effective measures for tackling these specific knots:

- perfectionism • fear of failure
- guilt feelings • worry and anxiety
- procrastination

Written in an upbeat, cheerful style, *Untying Your Knots* will encourage you to let God accomplish His good works in your life. And what about those problems that seem insurmountable? Fritz Ridenour writes these words of reassurance, "God's grace is sufficient. His power is made perfect in our knots." Learn to accept with loving trust the resources that God supplies for *Untying Your Knots*.

Untying Your Knots

Fritz Ridenour

Untying Your Knots

Power Books

Fleming H. Revell
Old Tappan, New Jersey

Unless otherwise indicated, Scripture quotations in this book are taken from the King James Version of the Bible.

Scripture texts identified NIV are from the Holy Bible, New International Version, copyright © 1973, 1978, 1984, International Bible Society. Used by permission of Zondervan Bible Publishers.

Scripture quotations identified NKJV are from The New King James Version. Copyright © 1979, 1980, Thomas Nelson, Inc., Publishers.

Scripture quotations identified PHILLIPS are from THE NEW TESTAMENT IN MODERN ENGLISH, Revised Edition—J. B. Phillips, translator. © J. B. Phillips 1958, 1960, 1972. Used by permission of Macmillan Publishing Co., Inc.

Scripture quotations identified LETTERS are from LETTERS TO YOUNG CHURCHES by J. B. Phillips. Copyright © 1947, 1957 by Macmillan Publishing Co., Inc., renewed 1975 by J. B. Phillips. Used by permission.

Scripture verses marked TLB are taken from The Living Bible, Copyright © 1971 by Tyndale House Publishers, Wheaton, Ill. Used by permission.

Scripture quotations marked NAS are from the New American Standard Bible, © The Lockman Foundation, 1960, 1962, 1963, 1968, 1971, 1972, 1973, 1975, 1977.

Acknowledgments continued on page 5.

Library of Congress Cataloging-in-Publication Data

Ridenour, Fritz.
  Untying your knots.
  Includes bibliographies.
  1. Christian life—1960–   . 2. Conduct of life.
I. Title.
BV4501.2.R523 1988   248.4   88-11532
ISBN 0-8007-1613-2

Copyright © 1988 by Fritz Ridenour
Published by the Fleming H. Revell Company
Old Tappan, New Jersey 07675
Printed in the United States of America

■ Contents

Untying Your Knots

ONE

▪ You Can Untie Your Knots If . . .

The first thing we must understand is that this is not a book about how to break up your marriage. If you have "tied the knot," I believe it's best to keep it tied. The knots I want to help you untie are spelled (k)nots, meaning the hang-ups and shortcomings we all accumulate in the process of living.

These knots come in all sizes and shapes:

- "I'm not as strong as I should be with the kids."
- "I'm not as loving and understanding as I ought to be with my spouse."
- "I'm not as confident and productive as I should be at work."
- "I'm not as faithful or godly as I should be."

You may have noticed that all these laments include the words *should* or *ought*. Almost every knot I have includes a should or an ought, and it's my guess that the same is true for you. In her book *Neurosis and Human Growth*, psychologist Karen Horney coined the term "tyranny of the shoulds." We get an idealized image of perfection in our mind's eye and tell ourselves: "I *should* be able to endure everything . . . I *should* be more understanding . . . I *should* like everybody and everybody *should* like me . . . I *should* be able to always be patient. . . ."[1]

Of course, none of us is that able, and the "should tyrants" tie us into all kinds of mental, emotional, and spiritual knots that turn into physical symptoms, as in "knots in the stomach" and other tender spots. Perhaps we identify best at the simple, everyday level where life's untidy ends seem to constantly pop out and knot up before we know it. Some of those untidy ends can be minor, like being Mother Witch all day long with the kids because of PMS miseries or becoming the growly Daddy Bear who preempts Mr. Rogers to watch a favorite bowl game. Nothing really horrible—no hitting, not even a lot of screaming—but the "should" feelings nibble around the edges and whisper, "You shouldn't act like this . . . You should be more loving and kind, understanding. . . ."

But for some, the untidy ends grow even longer and the knots become larger. Mom leaves for work after saying good-bye to her wailing two-year-old, who has just been dropped off at the day-care center. Dad trudges home at 9:00 or 10:00 P.M. after another fourteen-hour day on the corporate treadmill, only to find the children are all fast asleep. Tomorrow it will be more of the same: up and gone before they are awake and home after they're in bed. Who was it that said fathers spend less than three minutes a week with their kids? Or is it thirty-seven seconds? In too many cases the estimates are all too accurate and the guilt feelings all too real.

Kathy Grabbed Her Child's Throat

Sometimes life can unravel completely. The loose ends can become hopeless knots of incredible proportions. In her absorbingly honest book, *Out of Control*, Kathy Miller shares how she struggled to stop abusing her two-year-old daughter, who drove her to despair and rage with typical childish behavior. A sample:

"You went potty in your pants, I'll just have to spank you. I'll just have to spank you."

"No, no, mommy. I won't do it again."

"From now on you'll go on the potty chair. Do you hear?" Hitting her wet bottom and gritting my teeth, I grumbled, "I am sick and tired of wet pants . . . dirty pants . . . puddles on the carpet . . . loads of extra laundry . . . getting up in the middle of the night to change her soaking sheets."

My tortured thoughts ricocheted in my mind. *You're so much trouble. I can't do anything or go any place when I want. You demand love that I don't have. I don't want to be a mother!*

My hands grabbed for her throat. As if I were watching a scene from a horror movie, I saw myself choking Sandy. Her horrified face and fear-paralyzed body somehow satisfied me and I jerked my hands away. But I was terrified when I saw red marks on her neck. Suddenly, Sandy began screaming hysterically.

I ran out of the bathroom, making my way out the door to the back patio, I pounded my fists into my thighs and cursed myself. "How can I do this again? I've been doing so well. Oh, God, please help me. I'm out of control again."

Maybe I should call someone for help. If I called my pastor, I wonder what his reaction would be. I've never had any kind of therapy before. What would people think of me? How could I tell the ladies in my Bible study that I was going for counseling? They might not respect me anymore. They might think God doesn't have the answers. After all, if He hasn't helped me, they'll think He can't help them.[2]

Horror, shame, embarrassment, fear—all those knots were there for Kathy, along with a hangman's noose of guilt. How she freed herself from bondage makes suspense-filled, inspiring reading. You probably know someone with a similar story—not necessarily child abuse, but something just as serious or perhaps even more overwhelming and seemingly hopeless. For example, what *do* you do when you are a thirty-five-year-old divorcée who does an absolutely splendid job as a nursery worker at her church but who can't seem to say no when men invite her to bed?

"I know it's wrong," she tells her therapist. "But I'm so lonely—I just want to be *held!*"

All our knots cause us disappointment, disillusionment, self-reproach, guilt, anxiety, frustration, and even anger. We know we are not all we could be. We know we are not doing as well as we *should*—there's that word again.

We ask ourselves, why don't I seem to be able to change? Why can't I break my bad habits? What's so hard about mastering some simple rules of self-discipline that would make my life so much easier? Why doesn't my faith in God affect my life more directly? Sermons, services, Sunday school classes—they all seem so irrelevant to what I face all week long.

I believe change is possible. Habits can be replaced (not broken). Self-discipline does not have to be a tyrant. Most of all, faith in God can affect all of life. If He doesn't seem that relevant to you, maybe it's because He's a Gentleman who never bullies or barges in. He operates according to a different agenda called "grace." Scriptures say God is love and, as mind-boggling as that thought is, His grace is even more so. God's grace takes in everything—love, hate, sin, pride, pain, suffering, troubles—there is no knot His grace does not touch. And there is no knot His grace cannot unravel.

If grace means anything, it means that God is patient. He

keeps pouring love and forgiveness on us when we don't deserve it. Of course, we never did and never could. That's what makes it grace. Whatever we do to untie our knots, God's Grace Factor is at work, changing us into what He had in mind in the first place.

Are You Sure You Want to Untie Your Knots?

All that follows assumes that you *want* to change. A lot of people would rather live with their knots than start doing something about untying them.

Jesus found an invalid at the pool of Bethesda and learned that he had been lying there for thirty-eight years, hoping somehow to be the first one into the water when an angel stirred it up.

"Do you want to get well?" asked Jesus.

"Sir," the invalid answered, "if I just had somebody to put me into the pool when the water is all stirred up; but while I'm trying to get in, somebody always gets ahead of me."

The man's reply almost sounds like an excuse. He had no one to help him get into the healing waters of the pool at the right time. Had he lost hope or was he secretly content with his lot? Perhaps that is why Jesus asks the man what seems to be a superfluous question—does he want to get well?

But after thirty-eight years, perhaps the question is not superfluous at all. Perhaps the man almost prefers to live in his crippled despair. It's possible that he finds being an invalid has some advantages. If he gets well, he has to go back to work, earn a living, be up and at it every day.

A lot of people are like the crippled man at the pool. They continue with lives that are bound with knots that are pesky, irritating, or worse. They seem to have lost hope. They despair in ever doing much about untying them. For some people, their knots seem to be all that holds them together.

Their knots may be inconvenient, embarrassing, and even painful and destructive, but somehow they are comfortable because their knots are familiar. At least having knots seems safer than changing.

Jesus must have seen a spark of desire left in the man because He minced no words and simply said, "Get up, pick up your bed and walk!"

This story, which appears in John's Gospel, chapter 5, doesn't contain a lot of details. John's sparse account almost makes Jesus sound brusque, with little compassion. If we would reconstruct the scene today, we could imagine the man saying, "But I can't walk. Can't you see I'm crippled? I've been crippled for thirty-eight years! Besides, where will they mail my disability check? My lifetime invalid's pension? My Medicare benefits?"

But the Gospel account has the man making no protests. It only says, "At once the man recovered, picked up his bed, and began to walk."[3] New Testament commentator William Barclay speculates that it's as if Jesus told the cripple, "Let's do this thing together! You can get up if you try."

Barclay believes that, while we always must admit our own helplessness without God, we must still not neglect making our own efforts. ". . . in a very real sense," he writes, "it is true that a miracle happens when our will and God's power cooperate to make it possible."[4]

At first glance, Barclay's speculations prompt us to ask, "Is he trying to explain away a miracle done by Jesus? Is he saying Jesus didn't heal the man as much as He helped him make a supreme effort of which he thought he wasn't capable?"

Scripture clearly records that the Lord did many miracles—turning water to wine, making blind eyes see, and deaf ears hear, feeding five thousand with a little boy's meager lunch—and His divine powers are not in question. If we want to argue the point, a man who has been lying around for thirty-eight years would have absolutely no strength in his legs. Jesus miraculously healed those legs, but perhaps what Barclay wants us to fully grasp is that the man had to *believe* his legs were strong. He had to *make the effort* to get up.

Working with God to effect radical and lasting change makes sense. Jesus comes to every one of us, sees our knots, and asks, "Do you really want to be different? Do you want to be well?" From deep within each of us will come a very personal yes or no. If we are content to live with our knots, we will. As Barclay says, "The desire for the better things must be surging in our hearts."[5]

Out of that desire comes the will to "get up and walk," to do something about the knots that bind us. Without God we are helpless. When we trust His grace working in our lives, we gain strength to get up, pick up our beds, and walk!

Are Any of These Knots Yours?

By now you may be curious about the specific knots we will untie. I have chosen worry and anxiety, fear of failure, procrastination, perfectionism, and, last but really foremost, guilt feelings, which erode self-esteem. Some or all of these may be real knots for you, as they have been for me.

Worry and anxiety are often called "useless emotions" and so they are. Most people agree that being anxious and worried is a waste of energy, but they go right on doing it. If you're in my category of worrier, you don't go around muttering, "The sky is falling any minute now," but you do get anxious when there seems to be something to worry about, like a child or spouse who is overdue for dinner, or a stack of bills that is much higher than one slim paycheck.

Like most knots, worries and anxieties are very subjective. What worries me may not bother you at all, and vice versa. But what does bother us often ties us up and cuts down on our effectiveness and enjoyment of life. Is there a way to be "worry free"? Probably not, but there are ways to worry much less.

Fear of failure is a knot we try to deny with claims of self-confidence and bravado. No one climbing the Yuppie ladder to success would dare admit fear of failure. *Newsweek* may have proclaimed an end to the Yuppie era early in 1988,[6] but all the ladders are still up there and plenty of young, urban professionals are still trying to climb them. So are plenty of older professionals and not a few amateurs. We *all* want to succeed at whatever we do.

Fear of failure immobilizes many people. They don't necessarily collapse in a blubbering heap, but they do collapse inside. They decide to just not try. Fear of failure is one reason churches beg in vain for volunteers to teach Sunday school classes, do calling, or other ministries. Fear of failure keeps the junior executive a junior executive even though he or she has more smarts than the top brass in the company. Fear of failure keeps us from making that phone call, sealing that commitment, or inviting that new couple we've met over for dinner. We all fear failure, and strangely enough, some of us even fear success, because after the success what do we do for an encore?

Procrastination is what psychologist Wayne Dyer calls "the most universal of all erroneous zones." Even if you're a "do-it-now" type, I'm sure we could rummage around and find some chores, projects, or plans that you're putting off until "later" or "the right time."

If you're like me, you may excuse procrastination by saying you're gathering energy for the big effort. Over the years I have procrastinated my way into and through several dozen book-writing projects, including this one. Procrastination is especially easy for a writer. After all, what better excuse than, "I just don't feel inspired today—I'll have to wait until the right time." There is, however, no cure for procrastination like the stark terror of a deadline. Deadlines make you produce whether you're inspired or not.

Is there anything procrastinators can do to overcome their problem? I believe there is a lot they can do, if they'll do it now, not later.

Perfectionism is a knot I have battled all my life. Perhaps it began by being an only child, which made me more susceptible to wanting to be perfect in order to please my parents and other adult role models. But you can be a perfectionist, no matter what your birth order. My friend, Dr. Dave Stoop, counsels perfectionists every day and did a sizable survey that revealed 80 percent of the respondents struggling with perfectionism in certain broad areas of their lives.

Perfectionists strain for self-imposed standards that are always just out of reach. They miss a lot of joy and satisfaction that could be theirs if they would settle for "average" or just plain "good enough." If you are quite sure you're in that other 20 percent who aren't perfectionistic, you may say perfectionism is a knot you don't have to worry about. Wrong. Even if you aren't a perfectionist, you undoubtedly live with one or work with several. Perhaps you work for a perfectionist. Perfectionism is a knot we all need to understand.

Guilt feelings entwine themselves around almost everyone in what I believe is the toughest knot of all. Who among us does not battle feelings of disappointment, disillusionment, or despair because all too often we don't do what we know is right, sensible, and productive and we can't stop doing what we know is wrong, stupid, and destructive.

As we will see, guilt feelings are not necessarily all bad. Without guilt feelings, human society would turn into an arena that would make the average jungle look like "Romper Room." The trick is to turn guilt feelings into constructive godly sorrow and use your guilt rather than let it abuse you.

I realize that you may have many knots other than those mentioned here. Nonetheless, these will do as "case studies" in the art of disentangling life. It may sound simplistic to talk about always computing the Grace Factor when dealing with life's problems and hang-ups. In truth, it is a hard lesson to learn, not only in one's head but, more importantly, in the heart. The writers of Scripture, not to mention Jesus, had much to say about the perils of self-reliance.

There are many good self-help books and tapes available. Beyond that there are competent counselors and therapists who add the much needed dimension of "community," about which more will be said later. But self-help only goes so far, and even professionally done therapy or counseling has its limitations—and dangers. The greatest danger is to unconsciously rule out God's all-encompassing grace and turn inward. Instead of looking for help from a transcendent God who broke into history to bring us desperately needed redemption, we wind up looking to ourselves while we ask God to bless our efforts. The difference is as vast as the chasm He spanned at Calvary.

Does this mean we must condemn self-help, pop psych, professional therapists, and so on, and rely only on regular Bible reading and prayer? To do that would be far worse than shooting ourselves in the foot. We would be putting a gun to our heads. All truth is God's truth. He works through the therapist or He works through the friend or spouse who speaks an encouraging word. He communicates through deep theological and psychological discussions as well as through pop psych and self-help paperbacks. His Grace Factor is not limited to any one denomination, viewpoint, or pet theory. As the Apostle Paul told the skeptical Athenian philosophers, it is in God ". . . we live and move and have our being."[7] And it is through God's grace we can live and trust and untie our knots.

TWO

▪ Does God Help Those Who Help Themselves?

Psychologists suggest there are two ways to attack any knot: 1. Think yourself into a new way of acting. 2. Act yourself into a new way of thinking.

When I use the word *thinking*, I include feelings as well. A common error is to separate thoughts from feelings, but how can they be separate? What I think of something is how I will feel about it. As we will see, what and how we think is crucial but, to finally untie any knot or make any real change in behavior, we eventually have to focus on acting differently.

Fake It 'Til You Make It

In his fine book *Making Things Right*, Dr. Paul Faulkner mentions the motto that members of Alcoholics Anonymous use to encourage one another: "Fake it 'til you make it."

They aren't encouraging one another to be hypocrites. What they're trying to say is, "Fake the feeling that you don't want to drink and do it one day at a time."[1]

Many psychologists and psychoanalysts have used this principle for years. O. H. Mowrer, a strong advocate of dealing with neurosis through behavioral change, said: "It is easier to act yourself into a better way of feeling than to feel yourself into a better way of acting."

William James, the master pragmatist who was recognized as an outstanding psychologist and philosopher, put it this way: "You don't sing because you are happy, you are happy because you sing."

In their book *Happiness Is a Choice*, Frank B. Minirth and Paul D. Meier advise focusing on your behavior. "You don't do what you do because you feel the way you feel—you feel the way you feel because you do what you do. . . . In other words, your actions (godly actions or ungodly actions) will determine how you feel."[2]

In other words, if I choose to act lovingly, even though I may not feel all that loving at the moment, the feeling of love and goodwill will follow. I've seen this happen in very simple, even mundane ways. Helping my wife, Jackie, clear the table isn't something I always like to do, but after doing it, I always feel more loving. Conversely, if I don't help and selfishly go off to watch TV or get back to my latest book, I feel less loving, not to mention guilty.

I also see this principle at work when I'm driving, especially at intersections. When I let someone else "go first" in a left-hand-turn situation, it may mean waiting through another red light, but I still feel good about doing it.

When I asked Jackie if the "fake it 'til you make it" principle works for her, she said, "Well, I don't like to think I'm 'faking it,' but I do know that, as a deaconess, I don't always have time to take a gift to a family with a new baby, or flowers to someone in the hospital, but when I do it feels good. I don't like typing manuscripts for you late at night to meet a deadline, but it pleases me to get it done for you."

Jackie also remembers that when our kids were in high school her actions often determined her feelings. Perhaps it was working on a project with Kimberly that she had to have done by the next day. Or giving our two basketball warriors, Jeff and Todd, back rubs and foot rubs after a long night on the hardwood, when she had already had a long day herself. "Those were the times," she says, "that I felt the most loving and close to all of them."

How Johnny's Mom "Acted As If"

Jackie's mention of our children, who are now married and working on families of their own, underlines a key point. Perhaps the best training ground for acting yourself into a better way of feeling is being a parent. While lunching with my psychologist friend, Kevin Leman, he told me about counseling a mother and her teenage son, whom we'll call Johnny. The boy came from a devout Christian home, and his parents were understandably upset when he ran away, something Kevin had predicted several weeks before it happened.

"Don't overreact," Kevin told the parents. "Don't call the police. Chances are, within forty-eight hours you're going to know just where Johnny is, or at least have a pretty good hunch."

Sure enough, almost on the button, forty-eight hours after Johnny left, another boy appeared at the door and demanded that Johnny's mother give him certain items Johnny wanted: a stereo, clothes, and the like. Mom smiled sweetly (though fighting back tears) and gave the lad the stuff, never asking a single question about her son.

Because the mother knew the boy who had come for

Johnny's things, it didn't take her long to track her son down. Johnny was alive, well, and even attending school! Six days after he ran away, he decided to come home. Mom played it to the hilt, just as Kevin coached her to do. She was low-key—no histrionics or tears.

Her first words were: "Hi. How have you been? Haven't seen you around for a few days."

His first words were, "What's to eat around here?"

"Oh, there's plenty to eat," she replied. "Listen, I've got to run. If anyone calls, tell them I'll be back in about an hour and a half."

This very unusual mother then got in her car and drove over to the local mall where she spent "the longest ninety minutes of her life" trying to continue "acting herself into a new way of feeling."

Later, Johnny's mother came home with several bags of groceries and made him his favorite dinner. There was no fanfare or any comments like, "I cooked this just for you, Honey." Nonetheless, it was still a nice way of saying, "I'm glad you're home."

Throughout the entire affair, Johnny's mother wasn't feeling as cool, calm, and accepting as she looked. Part of her wanted to belt the kid and another wanted to scream, "DO YOU KNOW WHAT YOU'VE PUT US THROUGH?" But acting calm and nonjudgmental paid off. Not only did she feel better, but so did he and they were able to make real progress in their relationship.

Dr. George Crane, whose syndicated column containing homespun psychological advice appeared for years in newspapers across the country, sums it up when he says: "If you go through the motion, you will feel the emotion."[3]

Behaving your way into feeling better is what Paul Faulkner calls the "act as if" change agent. He often suggests it to married couples who are not getting along: "I want you to work at acting like a happy couple. Whether you feel like it or not, just act that way." More often than not, their relationship improves. By "acting as if," you can transcend and transform your own nature—you can do what's unnatural until it becomes natural.[4]

"Acting As If" Isn't Always Easy

It all sounds rather simple, and if everybody could do it, this book might end here. But there is always a hitch. Just how do I make that decision to "act as if"? Where do I find the motivation to go through certain motions even though I feel totally the opposite? My decision depends on what's really important to me. I might call these important things my priorities or, if I want to be a bit more technical, my values. Whatever I call them, whatever I do always mirrors who I really am.

If something is not that important, I will have a tough time "acting as if" it is. It is here, in the arena of my own soul, that I have to do battle with two little fellows who cause "cognitive dissonance." When I suffer from cognitive dissonance, it is something like thinking in stereo, with one speaker drowning out the other. One voice tells me to be responsible, consistent, and obedient to my values; the other attacks my values and says, *Come on, think of yourself for a change . . . relax . . . live a little.* Or perhaps the dissonance coming from my anti-values voice says, *You'll never do it . . . You don't have what it takes . . . Nobody likes you . . . Forget it. You're a loser.*

In his letter to the Philippians, which starts out as a thank-you note and turns into a masterpiece on knot-free living, the Apostle Paul speaks of how God works in us ". . . to will and to act according to his good purpose."[5] When Paul wrote those words, he was chained to one of Caesar's praetorian guards, under house arrest in a Roman prison. Nero was sorting out his options, which included cutting off Paul's head. Paul's intense personality had kept him tied in his own share of knots and we could understand if he had sounded a bit down and defeated in this kind of situation. Instead, his favorite words throughout his letter to Philippi are *joy* and *rejoice*. Whatever God decides to do is fine with him.

Does God Always Use the Red Sea Approach?

The Bible is full of scenarios where the principals are left waiting for God to do something. Moses, for example, got to the shore of the Red Sea, but he and approximately 2 million other Israelites didn't go any farther until God parted it. So, does God use the Red Sea approach in helping us change and untie our knots? In some cases I believe He does. God isn't limited to any one approach to doing anything, hard as we may try to box Him in. There are times when He reaches down and grabs somebody by the "scruff of the neck," but I believe His usual method is to give us some instruction, maybe a pep talk or two, and then let us try our hand at undoing our knots ourselves. He doesn't abandon us; He is still working in us to do and to will His good pleasure but, as Paul also wrote, He wants us ". . . to work out the salvation that God has given you with a proper sense of awe and responsibility."[6]

In other words, it's a reciprocal or two-way operation. Before Moses led the children of Israel through the Red Sea, he had been a fugitive from justice, content to herd sheep on the back side of the desert. One day God stopped him with a burning-bush greeting and told him he was to leave his tranquil life and return to the bright lights (and gleaming swords) of Egypt to inform Pharaoh that he must let all that free slave labor go.

"Who, me?" squeaked Moses. "I don't even talk so good—I couldn't do it. It's just not my thing."

"I know all that," God responded, "but I'll help you. In fact, I'll get Aaron, your brother, to be your backup. He speaks very well."[7]

That was it. A humble shepherd is given an assignment that would equal telling you or me to drop by the Kremlin and suggest that all the guests in the Gulag Hilton be given the option to leave. Did Moses really feel or think he could do it? I doubt it. But that didn't keep him from changing. He accepted God's offer of help and changed from a fugitive on the run to a dynamic leader because he acted upon a completely life-changing idea. A nonleader going nowhere became the guiding force of the greatest escape in history because he acted himself into a new way of thinking.

Now you may want to quibble about things like Moses' natural temperament, which had shown plenty of leadership qualities when he was younger. Or you may want to bail out and say, "That was fine for Moses, but he had God backing him up and even talking audibly to him. Some people claim God talks audibly to them, but I'm not one of them."

It's okay if you want to quibble. I quibble about these things, too, but that doesn't make the principle any less valid. If you're willing to act a different way, it can result in thinking and feeling a different way.

Is "Acting As If" Hypocritical?

If you want to quibble a bit more, you can ask, "Is acting differently in the hope of feeling differently hypocritical?" I suppose it's possible to see it that way. A hypocrite is someone who wears a mask and plays a role. But a hypocrite is also a phony who is trying to deceive people in order to gain unfair advantage or hide something that is wrong.

It's ironic that so many people want nothing to do with the church because it is "full of hypocrites." Yes, there are some hypocrites in any church, but there are far more people who want to act a certain way because they believe the Bible and have faith in God's power to change them. They may not be doing a very good job of acting out this different kind of role, but they are motivated by sincerity, not hypocrisy. They are doing their best to follow Paul's advice and work out their salvation with reverence and awe, all the while trusting God to work in them to accomplish His ends.

We see Paul's formula working in the life of Moses. Although he did not enjoy the full-blown grace that Paul experienced through Jesus Christ, Moses knew full well that his salvation rested in trusting God's love and mercy. And he worked out that salvation as he trusted God not simply to "help him," but to accomplish His purposes and His will.

According to the old cliché, "God helps those who help themselves." More correctly, God helps those who realize they need His help and are willing to move forward and act on that belief.

What we must be clear about is what we really believe. To repeat positive slogans, or even creeds and doctrines, is really quite easy. But what we really believe is revealed in our self-talk—how we think all day long. Your self-talk has a powerful effect on your feelings and how you will act.

In other words, both approaches are needed to untie our knots: We can act ourselves into a new way of thinking and feeling; and we can think ourselves into a new way of acting. It isn't an either/or. It is all *one*, as we will see in the next chapter when we grapple with the knot of worry.

In Summary

1. Become aware that the "tyranny of the shoulds" ties us in countless knots, as in "I'm not doing (or being) what I should."

2. Change is possible; there is no knot that can withstand God's Grace Factor.

3. Some people prefer to live with their knots, because they somehow feel safer, more secure and together.

4. To change means working with God, not waiting for Him to untie your knots.

5. The greatest danger in untying knots is to rule out God's grace, look inward, and try to "do it yourself."

6. God still works in wonderful, unlikely ways. In His grace we live and trust and untie our knots.

7. There are two ways to attack any knot: A. Think yourself into a new way of acting; B. Act yourself into a new way of thinking.

8. What and how we think is crucial but, to finally untie any knot or make any real change in behavior, we eventually have to focus on acting differently.

9. "Fake it 'til you make it" is not hypocrisy, but sound strategy for change.

10. To "act as if" takes motivation, which comes from your values.

11. Cognitive dissonance—two conflicting voices—keeps us struggling between living our values or violating them.

12. God works within us for His own pleasure, as we work out our salvation with awe and a sense of respectful responsibility toward Him.

13. To "act as if" is faith in action.

14. God helps those who realize they need His help and then rely on Him.

THREE

▪ Halt! What Worrisome Thought Goes There?

A supposedly true story tells of a hobo who hopped a freight and somehow got locked inside a refrigerator car overnight. *What will I do?* he wondered. *It's too cold to survive in here.*

The next morning they found his body inside the refrigerator car. Although the cooling mechanism had been shut off and the temperature in the car never dropped below fifty-four degrees, the man died, convinced he was freezing to death.

The hobo's fate is a dramatic illustration of a sage observation by Epictetus, a stoic philosopher who lived around 100 B.C.: "Men are disturbed, not by things, but by the view they take of them." About two hundred fifty years later, another stoic thinker, Marcus Aurelius, became emperor of Rome. One of "the last of the five good emperors," Marcus was best known as author of *Meditations*, a collection of his wise observations on life which includes this epigram:

> Take away thy opinion, and then there is taken away the complaint, "I have been harmed." Take away the complaint, "I have been harmed," and the harm is taken away.[1]

In other words, Marcus saw the same thing Epictetus saw: How we feel is not determined by our circumstances, but by what we *think* of our circumstances. How knotted-up—or how loose—you are depends on how you view what's happening in your life. What you tell yourself—your self-talk—will determine how you feel and how you act.

Self-Talk: As Easy as A, B, C

In *Self-Talk: Key to Personal Growth*, Dr. David Stoop explains our thinking process with the "A-B-C's of the emotions."[2] The A stands for "activating events" in our lives—that is, our environment or circumstances. In short, A is what happens to us. Our reaction to these activating events is C—the emotional/behavioral consequences. In many people, their natural reaction is to blame an activating event (their circumstances) for how they feel or act. When they limit their thinking to only these two steps, they come up with the equation $A = C$.

For example, suppose I phone you and you do not return my call. For me that's an A—an activating event. If I use $A = C$ thinking, I will wind up feeling hurt and rejected. I will simply blame my circumstances and feel accordingly. Some other examples of this $A = C$ thinking include:

A (I got a D on my test)	=	C (I'm stupid and dumb)
A (Sally didn't invite me)	=	C (I'm ugly and lonely)
A (I didn't get a raise)	=	C (I'm going to lose my job)
A (The kids are fighting again)	=	C (I'm a lousy parent)
A (She won't stop yelling at me)	=	C (She makes me so angry)

But what about *B?* When we leave *B* out, we are forgetting our A-B-C's. The *B* stands for belief system, which is another term for self-talk, what we tell ourselves because of what we believe. When we allow our belief system to work negatively, this is what happens:

Let's go back and use the unreturned phone call as the activating event. When my negative belief system takes over, I tell myself things like: "They don't want to talk to me." "They don't like me." "They're too busy for me." "Obviously, I'm not very important."

The consequence of this negative kind of self-talk is that I feel rejected and hurt.

A biblical way to describe the $A + B = C$ approach is Proverbs 23:7, "As a man thinketh in his heart, so is he." The trick is to turn negative belief system self-talk into positive input. Many passages in Scripture encourage gaining self-control by taking charge of your thoughts. In a letter to the Corinthians, Paul speaks of taking ". . . captive every thought to make it obedient to Christ."[3]

In one of the two letters he wrote to persecuted Christians who had plenty of reason for negative self-talk, Peter said, "Prepare your minds for action; be self-controlled; set your hope fully on the grace to be given you when Jesus Christ is revealed."[4]

Quoting Scripture is a powerful way to change your self-talk to positive, because it is a declaration of faith. As David Stoop observes, no one is faith*less:* "It is not a question if we possess faith or not. It is rather a question of where we place our faith. In our self-talk, our thoughts are the best barometers of the object of our faith. It is a process that works in releasing life-changing power in either a positive or a negative direction."[5]

Worry Is the Knot of "What If?"

One good way to check my self-talk and the object of my faith is to observe what's worrying me. If I worry about money,

I am admitting I really trust money. If I worry about my spouse leaving me, I really trust in my spouse. If I worry about losing my job, I'm trusting in my job for my well-being. Worry is the knot of "what if. . . ."

"What if I get sick and can't work?" "What if my children are stolen at the supermarket?" "What if my spouse has an affair?" "What if I get cancer?" "What if I have a heart attack?" "What if they drop The Bomb?"

Although it's called one of the most useless pastimes, worry is one of the most widespread. Probe very deeply under the brave facade of self-confidence worn by your friends and you will find their list of worries and anxieties. Oh, they may not like that word—*worry*—preferring instead, *concerns*, or maybe *things I'm praying about*. It's good to define terms when you talk about worries, and the dictionary describes two basic kinds of worrying: 1. You can worry something or someone else (as in "the dog worries the bone"); 2. You can be worried yourself as you "feel uneasy about some uncertain or threatening matter." *Worry* is also defined as "mental uneasiness or anxiety," and it includes the idea of "working under difficulty or hardship—to struggle." If you trace the word way back to its Old English source, you'll find it means, "To seize by the throat, to harass, or to strangle."

To be worried, then, means you are allowing something or someone that you perceive is a source of uneasiness or a threat to harass you, make things hard, and turn life into a struggle. No wonder worry and "what if" go together like hot dogs and baseball, or popcorn and a movie. The moment we ask, "What if?" we put something or someone in control of how we feel.

Worry Is Concern Out of Control

Yes, we know worry is useless. Psychologist Wayne Dyer says, "There is nothing to worry about! Absolutely nothing.

You can spend the rest of your life, beginning right now, worrying about the future, and no amount of your worry will change a thing."[6]

Dyer is right, of course, but that doesn't automatically turn off the worry button. The worry button doesn't shut off because we don't just worry about inconsequentials and unimportant things. We usually worry about things we care about, or at least think we care about.

Dave Stoop believes that the line dividing worry and anxiety from care and concern is hard to define. "Concern," he says, "can be defined as a feeling that motivates us to action. Worry, on the other hand, paralyzes us. Concern focuses on controllable behavior and events; worry focuses on events and behavior that are beyond our control."[7]

Dave's differentiation between worry and concern is helpful, but he has admitted to me in personal conversation that it's a fine line to walk. Caring can suddenly and easily become worry.

One of my "caring-turn-to-worry-knots" is getting concerned about members of my family who may be late getting home, especially if they have ventured out into Los Angeles's freeway system. Our freeways used to pose one basic threat— the strong possibility of accident, but all that changed a few months back when Angelinos made headlines around the nation by turning their freeways into shooting galleries.

Shooting incidents lasted awhile and then abated, but, of course, they can start up any time, as gridlock grips Los Angeles's freeway fighters a little more tightly every week.

Meanwhile, I still worry, er, get concerned, when Jackie goes out on weekly shopping and errand forays. If she's going to be late, I ask her to call, and if she doesn't, I start to pace as my writer's imagination clicks into gear. Using the A-B-C's of emotion approach, my thinking goes like this:

A (activating event)—Jackie's late. *B* (belief system)—

she's had car trouble, been in a wreck, assaulted in a dark parking lot, or . . . ?

All this leads to C (the emotional consequences)—I am worried to death!

I Become a Card-Carrying Worrier

While I was having lunch with my good friend, Norm Wright, who specializes in marriage counseling, I started sharing the concepts of this book and some of the knots that I have been trying to untie over the years. As we talked, I told him about my tendency to worry, including Jackie's frequent shopping trips on Los Angeles freeways.

"If she doesn't get home by a certain time, I start remembering every freeway murder and mayhem story I've ever read, and when you live around Los Angeles, that's a lot of mayhem! Not long ago, Jackie, my daughter Kimberly, and Kimberly's three kids drove out to Palm Springs for a few days of vacation in a condo we had rented. I had to stay behind to finish up some work and was going to come out later. But when I tried to phone them to see if they had arrived safely, there was no answer. At first I thought they might have stopped to buy a few supplies. But when a couple more calls got no answer, I started thinking about car trouble. After trying for about two hours, I finally got through. It turned out that the phone in the condo unit wasn't ringing, although I could hear it "ring" at my end. By that time, I had imagined just about every possible horrible fate that might have befallen all of them and I was ready to bring in the Highway Patrol."

"Did I hear you say your book also included some work on perfectionism?" Norm asked. "Perfectionists always see the glass of life as half empty. They automatically take a negative view, and this usually goes back to the perfectionist's strong need to be in control. The perfectionist has the overwhelming tendency to depend on himself and no one else. When you don't know where Jackie is or what time she'll be home, you're not in control, and that's why you get so worried."

"Well, what can I do to break this worry cycle?" I wanted to know. "Obviously, there's a little more to it than telling yourself, *It's going to be okay.*"

"Well, actually that's the bottom line. What you are battling is the same thing everybody else battles. I counsel people like this all the time. What happens is that your self-talk is negative. You've got to learn how to break that automatic, negative cycle and inject some positive thoughts that have more power."

"What do you mean, automatic negative self-talk?"

"By automatic, I mean that you're not deliberately talking worry-talk to yourself. You don't tell yourself: *Now I'm going to be negative and get worried.* Instead, it's just your habit. It all goes back to your glass-half-empty view of life. I can think of several ways you worry-talk to yourself. I'm sure you probably personalize a great deal. You think, *It all depends on me. It's all my fault. Why didn't I think of that?*"

"Well . . . I suppose I do tend to get on my own case quite a bit. . . ."

"Another thing you probably do a lot of is jump to conclusions. Jackie is late so you jump to the conclusion that something terrible must be wrong. And still a third habit that probably fits you is catastrophizing—*Something terrible is surely going to happen or may be happening already!*"

"You've got me pegged pretty well with all of those," I admitted. "But what can I do?"

"Well, there's a lot of data and all kinds of therapy techniques for people who worry and are anxious," Norm replied. "But what works best with my clients is very simple. I have them become 'card-carrying worriers.' "

"Is this a Gold Card? How much is it going to cost me to get one?"

"No charge—just buy lunch. Take a plain three-by-five-inch card and print on one side in big letters: *STOP!* On the other side, print in large letters at the top *THINK!*, and then print or type in a Bible verse like Philippians 4:6–9."

"Pardon my candor, but this sounds awfully simplistic—"

"Actually, it's a form of therapy based on very solid principles. I tell the client to keep the *STOP/THINK* card handy and every time there is a crisis or worry situation, take it out and use it."

"What do you mean by 'use it'? Is there some special technique or secret?"

"Not really. If no one is around, I suggest literally saying the word *stop* out loud and reading the Scripture passage aloud as well. Of course, if people are nearby, you can do all this silently—otherwise they might think you're just a little odd."

"I know Scripture is a powerful force, particularly in the life of the believer, but this almost sounds like a gimmick."

"I've had some clients say that at first, and then they find out how powerful this technique really is. I have seen many patients literally turned around by using this card. They worry a great deal less, and some have learned to not worry at all. My guess is that there are thousands of card-carrying worriers out there who are worrying a lot less because they remember to stop and think about what those verses say."

"Okay, I see your point. I think I'll try your card technique and see what happens."

So I did. I became a card-carrying worrier and have used the *STOP/THINK* technique with varying degrees of success. Some worries are easier to stop than others. Perhaps that is why worry and anxiety are the major mental problems of our time.

Ordinary human beings worry about their health, their

weight, their money, their appearance, their jobs, their safety, their happiness, the happiness of loved ones, being too young, getting too old, doing the right thing, and being loving enough. The list is endless and, as Wayne Dyer points out, the most neurotic worry of all is worrying about nothing to worry about. As someone in the seminar told him: "I can't just sit still when everything seems all right. I worry about not knowing what will happen next."[8]

But just why do we worry so much? Dyer gives some clues in *Your Erroneous Zones* when he lists several psychological payoffs for choosing to worry.

One big payoff is that worry gives us an excuse to put off something that may be pressing us at the moment. Instead of focusing on the deadline or task that needs doing now, I worry about something that might happen in the future. Worry always concentrates on something we fear may happen in the future, so it makes a perfect escape for the pressures and responsibilities we face at the moment.

Dyer confesses that he once put off the discipline of writing a book on counseling by worrying about his seven-year-old daughter's safety. He had gone out of the country to teach for the summer and write the book as well, during his free time. But every time he spun a sheet of paper into the typewriter, he thought of little Tracy Lynn back home. Was she riding in front of a car on her bike? Was she safe while in the swimming pool where she tended to be careless? Before Dyer knew it, he had spent an hour worrying, but it was "worth it," because as long as he could use up the present moments by worrying, he didn't have to struggle with the difficulty of writing. In his words, "A terrific payoff, indeed!"[9]

Dyer says worry is also a great excuse for procrastinating, being lazy, not taking risks, or not trying to change. A favorite excuse is that you "just can't do a thing" because you're so worried. Or perhaps you mask your worry as being cautious about going ahead with something too fast. But the payoff is always the same. You avoid risk, the pain of possible change, and getting out of your comfort zone.

One payoff that fits my "crisis at the condo" story is that worry makes you a caring person. By getting in a tizzy over my inability to reach Jackie, Kimberly, and her children, I could see myself as the good husband and father, as well as a loving grandfather to boot! Dyer notes this is a handsome payoff, indeed, although it lacks logical, healthy thinking.

Another big "payoff" for worrying is that it can cause all kinds of ailments—ulcers, headaches, hypertension. The pain and discomfort are worth it because of all the attention and sympathy I might get. Besides, all this ill health is a great excuse to throw pity parties and keep on worrying, which, for some strange reason, is more fun than good health and peace of mind.[10]

All these payoffs for worry are one big reason we develop the habit of automatic negative thinking. The best way to loosen our worry knots is to challenge that negative thinking. In other words, *you* call the shots. Don't let your habit of talking worry-talk control you.

There is a great story about Bill Klem, one of the most colorful big league umpires who ever called a ball and strike. Klem was known for his powerful, aggressive, "totally in charge here" style behind the plate. In a crucial game with a runner on third, the batter lifted a fly ball to left. As the ball settled in the left fielder's glove, the runner broke for the plate. Ball and runner arrived at the same moment and there was a horrendous collision.

Players in one dugout yelled, "SAFE," and the other side yelled, "OUT!"

As the dust cleared, Bill Klem stood above the plate, arm upraised, and shouted back for all to hear, "He ain't nothin' 'til I've called it!"[11]

Next time you have an automatic negative thought, tell that thought, "You ain't nothin' 'til I've called it." That's what the *STOP/THINK* technique is all about. In the next chapter, we will look at some practical additional ways to *stop* and *think* instead of letting worry and anxiety tie us in knots.

FOUR

■ Stop, Think, and Trust

While I was having breakfast with a good friend, I asked him what currently was worrying him, if anything. Because he's a very positive type, I expected him to say, "Not much." Instead he opened up about being very concerned at the moment about his son, whose marriage was in trouble because he couldn't seem to stick to any particular job very long. My friend also mentioned his retirement plans and wondering if he'd have money enough when it was time.

Worries can be short-range or long-range, but they always have to do with the future. What will happen—in the next few hours, next Friday, a month from now, ten years from now? Because we fear and dislike the unknown, our automatic reaction is to think negative thoughts about what we can't foresee. When we have these automatic negative thoughts we can tell them, "You ain't nothin' 'til I've called it," but just how do we call it?

The *STOP/THINK* card Norm Wright described to me at

lunch is a good start. When worries and anxieties persistently plague your thoughts, Norm also suggests wearing a rubber band loosely on your wrist and snapping it lightly when the worries come. The slight sting reminds you to *STOP/THINK* of what your negative thoughts are doing to you.

To expand on the *STOP/THINK* concept,[1] Norm shares some practical questions to ask when challenging negative thoughts.

In many situations it helps to start by asking: *What are the facts and what is my source of information?*

A lot of our worries are based on what we have imagined, not the facts. When we bother to get the facts from reliable sources, we will have a lot less to worry about—maybe nothing.

An excellent question to ask when worried about a loved one who's late getting home or some similar situation is, *What are the odds that what I'm worrying about may occur?*

Granted, it is possible that your loved one could have an accident or be harmed in some way, but just realizing that the odds against these tragedies are far greater than the chances that they will happen will help you control your worry.

A similar question is, *Am I borrowing trouble?*

Rita Davenport, a Phoenix, Arizona, talk show hostess who also does seminars and workshops to help women manage stress, suggests what she calls the "Scarlett O'Hara" technique for handling pressure and worries. In the film *Gone With the Wind,* Scarlett made famous the line, "I'll think about that tomorrow." Scarlett was a shrew, but she had a real point.

Rita Davenport tells women in her seminars about how fighter pilots are trained: "The instructor tells the recruits that they can think about going up in their planes, that the plane could crash, that they could be shot down, that their parachute could fail to open, and even if it did, they could get down to the ground and still be shot. The point is, why worry about any of that? Don't worry about anything until you face it. Most of what we worry about doesn't happen anyway."[2]

Scarlett O'Hara wasn't the first to talk about "thinking about that tomorrow." Jesus was almost two thousand years ahead of her when He said, "Therefore do not worry about tomorrow, for tomorrow will worry about itself. Each day has enough trouble of its own."[3]

A good question for the automatic, negative thinker is always, *Is my glass* really *half empty?*

When you ask this question, you are making yourself aware that you tend to think negatively, that you normally see situations as problems, imminent possible dangers. By stopping yourself and realizing that the glass could very well be half (or even more) full, you can stop worry in its tracks.

It also helps to ask yourself, *How relevant is all my worrying about this?*

Ironically enough, a lot of worrying isn't very relevant. It simply doesn't pertain to what's really going on in your immediate situation. Worrying about the problems of the world, world hunger, the high crime rate, and so on, are all irrelevant ways to waste your energy and get depressed. Instead of worrying about world hunger, contribute to one of many organizations or church efforts that are being made to alleviate it. The best way to turn useless worry into useful concern is to take some specific action.

Another counter to worry talk is, *Am I being too hard on myself—or maybe too hard on others?*

Several years ago, a husband-and-wife team of psychotherapists wrote a best-seller called *How to Be Your Own Best Friend.* The title sold the book as much as the content, which simply stressed not being so hard on yourself, not criticizing yourself, or putting yourself down. In other words, don't destroy your own self-esteem, build it up. There are plenty of others around who will try to destroy it for you.

Instead of worrying about how you might blow the sales presentation or the brief speech for your study group, think about the times you have been successful. Instead of asking, "What if I blow it?" simply say, "I did it well enough the last time, I'll be even better this time!"

What is my goal in doing all this worrying? is always a good worry-stopper. It immediately reminds you that worrying has no real goal. As someone said, "Worry is stewing without doing." It gets you nowhere.

Norm Wright asks many of his clients this same question over and over again: "What do you want?"

As you think about what you want out of life and how you want it to be different, it helps control and eliminate your worries. Focusing on a specific, reachable goal is one of the best ways to relieve or eliminate worry.

To flush out the fear that has you worried, ask yourself, *How would I act if I weren't worried* or *How would I approach this situation if I thought I could handle it?* We do a lot of worrying because we don't think we will be able to handle a certain responsibility or challenge. In any case, just thinking about how you could handle the situation will dissipate your worries and make you more confident.

Linked closely to the *How would I act if. . . ?* question is *What can I do about this?* Could I try a different approach? Am I willing to try *any* approach or do I just want to continue to wallow in worry because I'm getting some kind of psychological payoff that is better than attempting to take action?

And sometimes it helps to ask, *Why am I asking all these unanswerable questions?* Much worrying is done because we just have to ask "Why?" As in *Why did this have to happen? Why do I always have to have such rotten luck? Why me?*

Another favorite kind of unanswerable question begins with "What if. . . ." *What if I can't do it? What if something terrible happens?*

A few years ago a study of fear was done at the University of Michigan and results showed that 60 percent of our fears are unwarranted, while 20 percent are already history and out of our control anyway. Another 10 percent are so petty they don't make any real difference. Of the remaining 10 percent of all fears, only 4 or 5 percent are real. And of those 4 or 5 percent we can really do something about half of them. If this study is correct, only 2 percent of our fears are worth stewing about at all, and if we can start doing and stop stewing we can handle those as well.

I haven't done any correlating studies nor do I know of any that have been made, but since fear and worry are usually different sides of the same coin, you could almost insert the word *worry* for *fear* and use these same statistics. At least 60 percent of our worries are unwarranted, 20 percent are already history and, if not already past events, they are things that are totally out of our control anyway. At least 10 percent of our worries are so petty they aren't worth our time or energy and, of the remaining 10 percent, only 4 or 5 percent are what we could really call justifiable and we should be able to handle most of those if we'll simply start thinking positively.

Denis Waitley's "Big Red F" Days

Denis Waitley is known as one of the foremost advocates of positive behavior in the country. Almost weekly, he travels the jet streams, crisscrossing the nation to speak one day to a group of General Motors vice-presidents and the next day to a convention of top real estate brokers. His story of how he began as a scrawny kid who used to chase golf balls off the practice tee for Gene Littler, went on to Annapolis and navy wings, then to the world of corporate consulting and fund raising for the Salk Institute for biological studies, and finally to professional speaker and seminar leader, is a study in loosening and untying a lot of knots, including fear and worry.

For twenty years Denis has shared his secrets in seminars everywhere. In 1978, his audio cassette program, "The Psychology of Winning," became the best-selling personal growth program of its kind in the world. I have talked with Denis about fear and worry and he shared his own unique approach, which is based on setting aside seven days each year to do nothing but worry and be afraid. He calls them his "F" days and schedules one approximately every seven or eight weeks.

"What are you saying?" I asked him. "That you take a day off every now and then to just sit around feeling worried and scared?"

"Not really," he laughed. "What I use one of my 'F' days for is slaying my dragons, not letting them scare me. On an 'F' day I try to list all the things that are currently sources of worry or anxiety or fear. I write down my current and future concerns and then try to list alternative choices in dealing with them."

"How about an example? What do you worry about on one of your fear days?"

"One of my favorite 'F' days is for Fitness, but instead of worrying about fitness I turn my fear day into plans for follow-through. I schedule my annual checkup, as well as my six-month dental appointments. I analyze what I have been eating to be sure I'm not slipping into bad nutrition habits. I also take stock at how I'm doing at aerobic exercise. By the time I'm through with my 'Fitness Fear Day,' I have followed through on turning my fears and worries inside out and I feel a lot better."

Denis also has other "F" days like "Family Follow-through" when he takes time to listen to the needs of his wife and children and schedule some special times that he might not ever arrange if he didn't take time for a Family Follow-through day. He has lots of other big red "F" days for "Finances," "Friends," "Future," and "Facilities." His wife, Susan, particularly likes "Facilities Follow-through day" when he goes over everything that needs fixing around the house.

How to Get the Most Out of Worry

Denis's "Big Red F" days aren't really unique. His plan is based on a principle many counselors use with people who worry a lot. Norm Wright suggests to some of his clients that they're really not getting enough out of their worrying and that they ought to schedule special times of the day when they could "just worry."

Norm tells some clients, "Look, you're telling me you're doing quite a bit of worrying during the day, but it seems to be rather sporadic, and you're not getting full benefit out of it. But what you should do from here on is every time you begin to worry, write down what you're worrying about on a piece of paper. Then set aside a worry time every day from four to four-thirty. When four o'clock comes, you can take out your list and just worry as hard as you can—give it all you've got. When it's four-thirty you can put your list away, walk out of the room, and you've done your worrying for the day. Now what do you think of that?"

One client told Norm, "I can't believe I'm paying you for this . . . it sounds like a put-on."

Norm responded, "I couldn't agree more. All I'm trying to do is get you to make a value judgment and realize that a great deal of the worrying you do is useless."

Why Worry Is So Exhausting

Along with being useless, worrying and being anxious are very tiring, because they are processes that turn you inward to rely only on yourself. Ours is the age of self-sufficiency, self-help, self-centeredness, and self-made success. Paradoxically, millions suffer the anxieties of low self-esteem, poor self-image, and self-condemning guilt. This shouldn't surprise us. Self-centered people have plenty to worry about. To trust no one but yourself may be self-reliance, but it's a lonely way to travel.

One of the telltale signs of self-sufficiency is impatience. We read condensed books and magazines—even condensed newspapers that give us the story in eight column inches or less—as we sip instant coffee and plan the next instant microwave dinner. *Wait* is a four-letter word. We don't want to wait. We want it now.

We extol patience as a virtue, but we find it hard to practice because we think it means we are to "do nothing"—just sit on our hands hoping something will happen. The scriptural meaning of patience, however, suggests an active process that you do with expectancy and hope. And instead of tiring you out, this kind of patience gives you new energy and strength.

The prophet Isaiah wrote to the impatient Israelites and said,

> How can you say that the Lord doesn't see your troubles and isn't being fair? Don't you yet understand? Don't you know by now that the everlasting God, the Creator of the farthest parts of the earth, never grows faint or weary? No one can fathom the depths of His understanding. He gives power to the tired and worn out, and strength to the weak. Even the youths shall be exhausted, and the young men will all give up. But they that wait upon the Lord shall renew their strength. They shall mount up with wings like eagles; they shall run and not be weary; they shall walk and not faint.[4]

When Isaiah mentioned "renewing strength," he used a Hebrew word that actually means "to exchange." When you patiently wait upon the Lord, you exchange your weakness for His strength.[5]

The Most Important Question of All

All the *STOP/THINK* questions in this chapter are examples of what counselors call "cognitive therapy." Using cognitive therapy techniques to *STOP/THINK* and challenge negative thought patterns is useful, but what happens when the *STOP/THINK* questions don't work? What happens when thinking about your goals or your source of information or how hard you're being on yourself only causes more stress and anxious feelings? Suppose you ask yourself, *How would I act if I weren't worried?* and you get back the answer, *How do I know? If I weren't worrying, I would be acting differently, wouldn't I?*

That's where the Scripture references on the *STOP/THINK* card come into play. They remind you to turn to a power greater than yourself, and ask, *Who do I really trust?*

Norm Wright recommends using Philippians 4:6–9 on your *STOP/THINK* card because it outlines the three stages of dealing with worry.[6] First Paul gives the *premise:* "Do not worry about anything" (*see* v. 6). And how do we achieve that blessed state? We have to *practice* more than cognitive techniques. We are to practice prayer. "In everything by prayer and supplication, thanking God for all that He is in our lives, we make our requests known to Him" (*see* v. 6).

Finally, we have the *promise*—"the peace of God that goes beyond our comprehension will guard our hearts and minds through the power of Christ Himself" (*see* v. 7).

These are powerful words. How do we keep them from turning into glib advice to "just pray about it—let go and let God"?

Paul's next sentence gives us some clues. He isn't saying, "Now stop your worrying. It's sinful and it shows that you have weak faith and don't really trust the Lord. If you'll just ask Him, He'll give you peace."

If we want peace, says Paul, we can think thoughts that will produce peace—thoughts that are "true, noble, right, pure, lovely, admirable, excellent and praiseworthy" (*see* v. 8).

Here Paul outlines a plan for changing our way of thinking. We must change our automatic negative thoughts that lack faith and trust and deliberately turn our faces toward God and His peace (v. 9). The old hymn is so right:

> *Turn your eyes upon Jesus,*
> *Look full in His wonderful face,*
> *And the things [worries, anxieties, etc.] of earth will*
> *grow strangely dim,*
> *In the light of His glory and grace.*

In Summary

1. Worries are caused by automatic negative self-talk. In other words, worry is a habit.

2. Worry is the knot of "What if?" As soon as you ask "What if?" you put something or someone in control of how you feel.

3. Worrying is useless, but a hard knot to undo because we usually deeply care about or for whatever or whomever we worry about.

4. People who need to be in control are especially vulnerable to worry. They tend to depend on themselves and no one else.

5. Worries always have to do with the future—with what might happen, much of which is out of our control.

6. We worry because there are psychological payoffs: It gives us an excuse to put off our responsibilities, to procrastinate, to think we are noble and compassionate, or to become ill, which gains us sympathy and attention.

7. A good way to stop worry is to challenge automatic negative thinking with a *STOP/THINK* technique. Some good questions to stop negative thoughts and think things through are these:

    a. What are the facts and what is my source of information?

    b. What are the odds that what I am worrying about may occur?

    c. Am I borrowing trouble?

    d. Is my glass really half empty?

    e. How relevant is all my worrying about this?

    f. Am I being too hard on myself—or maybe too hard on others?

    g. What is my goal in doing all this worrying?

    h. What do I want?

    i. How would I act if I weren't worried? How would I approach this situation if I thought I could handle it?

    j. What can I do about this?

    k. Why am I asking all these unanswerable questions?

    l. Who do I really trust?

8. The best question to help stop worry is "Who do I really trust?" Millions in our self-sufficient society believe, "You can only trust yourself," and thus ignore or neglect their most powerful resource.

9. A sure sign of self-sufficiency is impatience. We extol patience but don't practice it because we think it means sitting on our hands, hoping something will happen. The scriptural meaning of patience, however, is to hope actively and expectantly, waiting for God to renew our strength.

10. The following chart illustrates the difference between "worry-talk" and the kind of countering self-talk that can stop worry in its tracks.

Worry-Talk	Positive Self-Talk	Who Do I Really Trust?
She's over an hour late — something terrible must have happened!	*STOP! THINK:* Are you borrowing trouble? She's been late before. Traffic is heavy, but she's a good driver and is probably being extra careful.	"Do not be anxious about anything, but in everything, by prayer and petition, with thanksgiving, present your requests to God. And the peace of God, which transcends all understanding, will guard your hearts and your minds in Christ Jesus" (Philippians 4:6, 7 NIV).
Bills are piling up. We'll never get out of debt. We may lose our home!	*STOP! THINK:* Is your glass really half empty? What are your goals in worrying about this? How can you work with what you've got? What can you be doing instead of just stewing?	"And my God will meet all your needs according to his glorious riches in Christ Jesus" (Philippians 4:19 NIV).

| I worry about having my baby. What if it's born with something wrong? | *STOP! THINK:* What are the odds that something may be wrong? They are probably very small. How would you act if you weren't worried? | "Whatever is true, whatever is noble, whatever is right, whatever is pure, whatever is lovely, whatever is admirable—if anything is excellent or praiseworthy — think about such things . . . and the God of peace will be with you" (Philippians 4:8, 9 NIV). |

The above examples illustrate the difference between worry-talk and the kind of countering self-talk that can dispel worry and even drive it away completely. The most important question to counter worry is always, *Who do I really trust?* The most positive kind of self-talk is repeating God's promises from His Word.

FIVE

■ Nothing to Fear But Failure

What is the knot shared by more people than any other? According to some experts, the answer is "fear of public speaking," and I agree—for a good reason.

One of the most miserable failures of my life occurred when I was in a public speaking situation, and I wasn't even the main speaker! I was in my junior year of college and the occasion was a day-long meeting of editors of college newspapers from all over the Northwest. Part of the program was a panel discussion among several of the editors, which was led by a vice-president of a local public relations firm. I don't remember his name; I don't remember what the topic of the panel discussion was. But I have remembered vividly to this day what happened.

Mr. Smooth (let's call him that because he conducted the panel so skillfully) turned to me and asked a question. Up to that point I had not spoken. I should have quit while I was ahead. The question wasn't difficult—something in the range of my name and address—but I blanked. Then I froze in the clutches of sheer terror.

At first Mr. Smooth was puzzled and he tried to help me by
rephrasing the question in even simpler terms. It didn't help
at all. I stuttered, gurgled, and almost strangled. I never really
got out an entire, comprehensible sentence.

Every eye in the room seemed fixed directly on me. I felt
short of breath. I would have probably hyperventilated, but I
didn't know the meaning of the word. Perhaps I was hyper-
ventilating anyway, but I had no paper bag to breathe into, so
it makes no difference. Besides, if a paper bag had been
handy, I would have put it over my head.

Mr. Smooth kept looking at me, his puzzlement turning to
mild irritation (I was lousing up his panel) and finally to
deferential pity. With a "moving right along" phrase, he
deftly took the glaring spotlight off me and called on other
panelists. Somehow he never got back to me, which was just
fine with both of us.

But my faux pas weren't over. As the panel ended its work
and rose to its feet, I rose also, hastily because I wanted to get
out of there fast. Somehow I caught my foot in my chair, and
it flipped over with a crash. Once again, every eye seemed to
be on me. I mumbled an apology to no one in particular and
fled the room.

After that, I feared public speaking with total passion for
years. It wasn't simply getting up in front of people. As a winner
of eleven varsity letters in high school sports and recipient of
athletic scholarships to different colleges, I was "used to performing before the crowd." But somehow forming words and
phrases and speaking them coherently to an audience became
an incredible problem, which I trace back to the traumatic
moment when Mr. Smooth turned to Mr. Choke and asked
something along the lines of, "And what do *you* think?"

My problem was, I couldn't, and from that day I struggled with thinking and speaking in front of a group—any
group.

A lot of people don't understand this. A writer and editor should certainly have no trouble with words, right? Well, partly right. I have no trouble as long as the words are on paper. But when they are in my mouth, it is another story. I am afraid. I "edit" myself even as I am talking, which leaves me thinking in a sort of odd stereo fashion, my ears hearing what I say, while my brain wants to take a copy pencil to them almost before they are out of my mouth.

What Causes My "Lalophobia"?

The technical term for my fear-of-speaking malady is *lalophobia*, but I believe my real problem is fear of failure. Today I do public speaking and teaching, and particularly like the give-and-take of a discussion setting. But speaking still is hard work. Fear of failure haunts me and ties me in its own obnoxious, repugnant knot.

The truth is, I am afraid—afraid I will do a poor job, be dull, forget what I want to say, and, God forbid, not be able to utter more than gurgling sounds as I did before Mr. Smooth and my college peers over three decades ago.

Perhaps you have a "fear of failure" knot of some kind. Fear of failure is widespread and it keeps many people tied in knots of indecision, procrastination, and what appears to be inaction. Actually, the person who fears failure would like to act, but the risk is too great, the stakes too high. To fail is frightening, unthinkable.

Victim, Sustainer, or Dreamer?

Those who fear failure often play one of three roles: victim, sustainer, or dreamer. Victims live in the past, lamenting what might have been. Their favorite phrases are *should have, could have, might have,* and *if only.*

Victims gain sympathy with all kinds of excuses. They blame the traffic for running late. They blame the department upstairs for making their monthly report overdue. They blame the children for the house being a mess. "If only I could have married Roger," the victim wails. "If only my horoscope had been right today . . . If only I had been born rich . . . If only I wasn't stuck in this rotten job."

I am not discounting the many millions who have suffered terrible tragedy, illness, and persecution. Every day people are duped, swindled, cheated, lied to, and put down. News media call them "victims," but in truth they are simply people who have had bad things happen to them. It is their *response* that decides if they are victims or not.

Victims believe they are helpless. As Denis Waitley points out, "They see themselves as thermometers, controlled by external circumstances rather than as thermostats that can control their destiny."[1] And, of course, victims fear failure. Playing victim is a good way to hide from your fear. No one will fault the victim for not trying something. After all, the victim needs sympathy and help.

Marjorie comes to women's Bible study every week with a new tale of woe. The children have been sick; she has been sick. Her husband is insensitive and he may lose his job. The plumbing backed up, and so on, and so on.

"Poor Marjorie," everyone sympathizes. "Why her?"

Why not? Marjorie gets lots of attention and sympathy and is never asked to do anything but show up to play her victim role. There is nothing wrong with sharing a problem with your Bible study and drawing strength from their concern and prayers. But continually shouldering the burdens of a victim is emotionally unhealthy and spiritually defeating.

Sustainers Are Survivors

Sustainers put on a braver game face for the world than do victims. Sustainers are the champions of the status quo. They live in the here and now and think very little about the future.

Unlike victims, sustainers are survivors. They hang in there and learn how to go with the flow and roll with the punches.

"We've always done it this way, why change now?" "There is no need to go out on a limb." "Why fix what's working?" All these are favorite sustainer phrases.

George stays right where he is as assistant manager, even though he has been offered a head manager's job several times. George knows that being head manager would put him on the spot, force him into situations where he would have to make decisions and take risks. He'd rather stay right where he is. As assistant manager, he can play the role of the conservative who "knew we shouldn't try that one."

George is a sustainer who fears failure, but in another sense he fears success. Moving up to manager would be a "success" but it would also put him under pressure to produce. Fear of success is the flip side of fear of failure. After I succeed, what do I do for an encore? Can I do as well again? Can I do as well if I'm pressured to produce a little more and try a little harder? Better to stay right where I am and "sustain the status quo."

Dreamers Plan Voyages to "Someday I'll . . ."

Dreamers are the ones who talk a good game but seldom show up for the kickoff. They're always describing their goals and plans in grandiose detail. "Someday I'll . . ." say the dreamers, as they describe that magical place to which they will sail—someday. Someday we will write that book, fix that roof, knit that sweater, contact those friends we haven't seen in years, start that business, and so on, and so on.

You may recall seeing the TV commercial for a computer company which always shows an intense Yuppie type, who is in the shower, or possibly driving down the road on the way to a holiday or vacation. If we wish to identify with this strong, attractive person, we understand that we never take time off. Even in the shower, even driving toward a good time and a few good days of relaxation, we are thinking, always thinking. Suddenly the light dawns.

We jump out of the shower (or slam on the brakes) and rush to a phone. We call the office and our first words are: "Hello, Joe? Remember that McPherson account? Why don't we try this. . . ?"

The point is made. People who work for this particular company never rest, they're always thinking, always planning, always asking, "What about doing this . . . ?"

One reason this ad appeals to us is that it is the antithesis of the dreamer. We all can think of times when we lose ourselves in our dreams but never do anything about them. We admire anyone who goes into action and gets the job done.

Again, fear of failure lurks in the background. "Someday I'll . . ." is a much more attractive place than "Today I'll . . . ." To talk about doing something "someday" is safe. It's fun, it feels good, and it's painless. Dreams cost nothing. Doing, taking the risk, going out and playing the game costs plenty.

Victims, sustainers, or dreamers all fear failure, because their self-talk is tuned to a negative frequency. Because they are afraid to take a risk, they stay tied in a knot of fear, sure there is no way to escape. On the surface they don't appear to even want to untie their knots but, secretly, many victims would like to fight back, sustainers would like to be a little more bold and willing to take risks, and dreamers wish they could actually pull something off instead of just talk about it.

You may have played one or more of these roles at different

times. I know I have. There are, however, several ways to counter this kind of destructive self-talk and win.

How Do You Know It's "Failure"?

To begin untying the fear of failure knot, develop the habit of always putting failure in perspective. Since everybody fails, there is no point in feeling lonely. You have plenty of company. Rather than feel defeated, as if you are the only one with this problem, keep in mind that failure is only one side of the coin and on the other side can be success.

There is an ancient story about a Chinese landowner with a large estate. A herd of wild horses, worth a great deal of money, wandered onto his property and were captured. The land baron's neighbors congratulated him on his luck, but he replied, "How do you know I am lucky?"

A few days later the man's son, a strong youth who was a good horseman, tried to break one of the wild stallions. He was thrown, landed heavily, and broke a leg. The neighbors offered the landowner condolences on his misfortune, and this time he said, "How do you know I am unfortunate?"

A few weeks later, the king of the province declared war and all able-bodied young men were ordered to report for duty. The landowner's son, still on crutches with his broken leg, was exempted from the fighting, which claimed many lives. Again the neighbors commented on how fortunate the landowner had been. His answer? "How do you know I am fortunate?"[2]

The point of this enigmatic tale is that it is very hard to know for sure if you have had a good day or a bad one. Rudyard Kipling put it well when he spoke of failure and success and treating both those impostors just the same.

Another story about a Norwegian fisherman also illustrates how success and failure can be different sides of the same coin.

The old man and his two strong sons were out on their daily run with the nets. Their luck was good and as they hauled in what seemed like tons of fish, they failed to notice an approaching storm that hit them suddenly. Dark clouds and mountainous waves blotted out the shoreline and they were totally confused with no idea where to head for safety.

As the old man and his sons battled the elements and tried to get their bearings, another disaster hit back home. Fire broke out in their cottage and it burned to the ground. Hours later, the fisherman's wife, who had managed to escape the fire unhurt, saw her husband's little boat reach shore safely. Tearfully she told him and her boys that fire had destroyed their home.

"Karl," she cried. "What will we do? We have nothing left."

"We have our lives," Karl answered. "You could have died in the fire. I and the boys could have died in the storm. We were completely lost, but then I saw a glow—far away. We made for that light and somehow reached shore. That light was our home going up in flames and it saved our lives."[3]

It would have been easy for the old fisherman to join with his wife in playing the victim, but his self-talk—and his perspective—remained positive. And the principle is universal. Failure or disaster can be the bearer of good. It really does depend on how you look at it.

Lincoln Turned Failure Inside Out

Abraham Lincoln failed as a businessman and as a politician. He could have given up, become a victim, and lived out his days as a backwoods lawyer who just "never got the breaks." Instead, he became one of the greatest presidents in United States history.

Even Lincoln's assassin could not defeat him. The Union

for which he fought so hard remained intact, slavery was abolished, and the hatred and prejudice of racism was dealt a mortal blow.

Lincoln had many a bad day. He was often told that he was a failure who looked like a gorilla. He was considered a goon who had no class, who couldn't even speak with much eloquence.

On the day he presented his Gettysburg Address, Lincoln was preceded to the platform by a man who spoke with brilliance for over two hours. The newspaper commented on how beautiful and inspiring the first speaker's speech had been. And why not? This first speaker was a former president of Harvard. He had served as a United States senator, as well as governor of Massachusetts.

Today, however, no one can find a copy of Edward Everett's two-hour speech, which was hailed as such a success on the day he gave it. Lincoln's Gettysburg Address took three and a half minutes, and his critics called it a disgrace to the office of the president of the United States. Time has proved them wrong. The Gettysburg Address is studied and quoted by millions of school children and recognized as one of the most moving pieces of oratory ever uttered. On the day after the Gettysburg Address, Lincoln might have said to his critics, "How do you know I gave a bad speech?"

Sunday Always Follows Friday

And then there was the Carpenter whose itinerant preaching attracted too much popular attention and aroused the ire of the religious hierarchy who accused Him of blasphemy. Biding their time, they trapped Him with the help of a tip from a trusted friend and framed him with false testimony at a trial that was a kangaroo court. The Carpenter was executed and buried in a borrowed tomb. His followers scattered.

On that day, what might His mother or close friends have said? Had it been a "good Friday"? In the gloom and darkness that covered everything, Jesus' followers were yet to realize that Sunday and success were coming.

Into Every Life Some Failure Falls

A key to having the right perspective toward failure is to realize it is one of the most universal of all experiences. None of us achieves anything significant in life without suffering some failures and disappointments. In fact, we may suffer disappointments for years without having much success. We may fail again and again, hoping for the thrill of victory, but tasting the agony of defeat.

Gerhard Gschwandtner, publisher of the motivational paper, *Personal Selling Power,* became fascinated with studying the effects of disappointment and failure and how people can regroup and grow after suffering setbacks.[4]

Part of that study included a visit to the Library of Congress in Washington, D.C., to research the topic of "disappointment." He found over twelve hundred books devoted to the subject of success but only seventeen books on the subject of losing or failure. Gschwandtner was amazed to discover there were no books on disappointment and only one magazine article, "The Management of Disappointment," written by Dr. Abraham Zalenznik for the *Harvard Business Review,* sixteen years earlier.

When Gschwandtner and his wife, Laura, who serves as editor-in-chief of *Personal Selling Power,* visited him in his offices at Harvard University School of Business Administration, Dr. Zalenznik was surprised. It had been sixteen years since he had published his article, and they were the first people to show any interest in the subject of disappointment. Dr. Zalenznik believes a common misconception about disappointment is that it is always bad; therefore, it is never good to admit you are disappointed. Disappointment can't possibly have any connection with success.

"People see disappointment as a down," Dr. Zalenznik told the Gschwandtners, "and they don't want to be associated with anything that is not up and positive."[5]

Gschwandtner was to have firsthand experience of Dr. Zalenznik's wisdom. When he told people he was publishing an article on disappointment in *Personal Selling Power*, his friends said readers would be turned off and tuned out. But Gschwandtner's strong hunch was that people wanted to know how to improve their performance and that they are willing to deal with a subject like disappointment. What people needed to understand was that disappointment doesn't equal failure. It's what you do with disappointment that determines if you will be a failure or not.

Gschwandtner's hunch was right. The issue of *Personal Selling Power* in which the interview of Dr. Zalenznik appeared was a best-seller and reprints were ordered at a steady rate for many months.[6]

Disappointment and Disaster Make You Stronger

Dr. Zalenznik also observes that disappointment is inexorably linked to ambition. The more effective person is the one who has modified his or her ambitions but retained drive—the desire for mastery, competence, and excellence. There is a big difference between having drive and being driven. The person with "burning ambition" is usually impatient, torn, and restless. He or she wants to go through life making every green light and never having to take any detours.

But you can't make every green light and avoid every detour. No one travels all of life's journey without hitting some red lights or even getting hit by an absentminded soul who is fiddling with his radio.

On the other hand, you may be the one who fiddles around and causes his own detour as I once did. When I edited our college paper, we got a reputation for excellence and won "all-American" awards several years in a row. Our dedicated staff worked late many nights of the week, and on Thursdays I drove to the print shop to oversee final makeup of the paper, so it could be printed and distributed on campus the next day.

On one particular Thursday, I jumped in the car with a pile of last-minute copy that needed typesetting and headed for the print shop. As I zoomed away from one red light, I looked up to see a giant billboard with a clock and decided to check my watch against the clock to see if I was running late.

Checking my watch took only a few seconds, but by the time I looked up, I had traveled a short block to another stop light which had turned very red. Another car had already stopped in front of me. I hit the brakes hard, which only caused my bumper to slide under his. I bounced the car ahead of me out into the intersection with virtually no damage to it.

But when I tried to open my door, it would barely move because my front fenders were rearranged several inches toward the rear. I finally got out and surveyed what used to be my radiator and grill. Adrenaline had pumped my stomach full of butterflies, but as I looked at the mess, the butterflies turned to vultures. How could I get the paper out on time? How could I think straight enough to do *anything* on time?

Fortunately, the other driver was an understanding sort who did not cuss me out, attack me, or go looking for a lawyer specializing in whiplash. Somehow I got it all taken care of: a quick call to the print shop to tell them I would be a "little late," making out the accident report for the insurance company, having the car towed to a body shop, calling a friend who drove me over to the printer's. Once there, concentrating on proofreading and page layouts took my mind off the disaster that used to be an almost-new Plymouth coupe.

When disaster strikes, it's tempting to wring your hands, fold your tent, and quietly slide under a rock or into a hole. But failure isn't final unless you choose to let it have the last word. In fact, it can help you. In Nietzsche's words, "What does not kill me makes me stronger."

The Herald Was the Real World

You may not feel any tremendous increase in emotional muscles during moments of failure or disappointment, but there will be gain through the pain in the long run. Getting out my college paper on that day when I practically totaled my car was just one of many strengthening experiences that prepared me to absorb pressure and criticism out there in "the real world." A few years later I found myself working as news editor on a weekly paper in a small lakeside community just outside Minneapolis. My college newspaper experience was invaluable preparation for working at the *Herald*, where I quickly learned to do the work of two or three people in half enough time.

There was also plenty of heat from my very precise and demanding editor-in-chief, from irate city councilmen who threatened lawsuits for "misreporting" their meetings. And then there was "Evvy," a colorful veteran feature writer who called me exotic names every time I cut her social gossip column to make room for the ads that were the paper's lifeblood.

During the two years I worked at the *Herald*, I experienced numerous disappointments and failures. I was criticized, pressured, cussed out, constantly in a state of exhaustion. But I also had successes, a few compliments, and the satisfaction of getting the paper out every week. The journalism degree they handed me at graduation from college turned into a certificate of craftsmanship. Come to think of it, compared to those two

years I spent on the *Herald,* all my other jobs have been a
piece of cake!

The principles in this chapter make good philosophy, but
the missing element is a strategy for actions that will combat
the fear of failure and beat it. Chapter 6 talks about how you
can "act as if" and conquer fear. You begin by saying yes to
your fears as you learn to fail successfully.

SIX

■ How to Fail Successfully

Dealing with disappointment and failure takes positive thinking, but it also takes realistic thinking. A common mistake taught by some positive thinkers is that if you can believe something hard enough, it will happen. "This," says Dr. Abraham Zalenznik, "is pure idiocy." Somewhere along the line you have to develop talents and disciplines if you want to resolve your disappointments and fear of more failure.

Fears come in many shapes and sizes. As you know, one of mine is public speaking. Yours might be driving on freeways, confronting a cranky boss, drawing closer to a rebellious teenager, taking a new job, or making any decision more important than where to eat lunch.

Dr. Susan Jeffers, who has taught numerous courses on handling fear, believes it comes at different levels. In her helpful book *Feel the Fear and Do It Anyway*, she talks about surface-level fears that "just happen," like aging, the empty nest, going broke, getting seriously ill, or being in a car accident. At the same surface level, we also fear actions we have to take: making a telephone call, going to a job interview, and so on.

These "just happen" and "have to do it" fears spring out of more basic ones that affect the ego or self-esteem. Examples include being rejected, swindled, or crippled. Other examples of these broader fears are fear of rejection, vulnerability, helplessness, or disapproval.

At a still deeper level, says Dr. Jeffers, is the foundational fear for all the rest: *You just don't think you can handle what might happen.* You can't handle blowing the job interview. You can't handle being broke, you can't handle being rejected, or being vulnerable.[1]

In almost every case what you are saying is, "I can't handle failure. I can't handle blowing it, not making it, not being in control, feeling guilty and inadequate."

The Truth About Fear

To help people handle their fears, Dr. Jeffers bases her teaching and counseling on several basic truths that include:

1. As long as you try to grow and change, you will always have fear. In other words, as long as you're out there trying to take the tiniest risk or step toward conquering whatever it is that you're afraid of, the fear will be right there in your face. You can hide and sweep it under your psychological rug. You can tell yourself, *That doesn't bother me.* But the moment you try to step in the direction of growth or accomplishment, the fear will be there waiting.

2. The only way to deal with a fear is to go ahead and do or face what you are afraid of. As you take those tiny steps toward growth or change, you will feel much better, have more confidence, and have less fear.

3. You aren't the only one who is afraid. Everybody faces fears of some kind. All those self-confident types who seem to

do anything they want are grappling with fear, too. The difference is, they are grappling and winning.

4. It's more painful to live with fear and feeling helpless than it is to "push through" that fear and conquer it. In other words, "Why not?" is less frightening than "What if?" People who play the "What if?" game are knotted with fear. They don't want to take a risk or any steps that might take them out of their comfort zone. People who say "Why not?" are willing to take that risk and usually discover that stepping out of one comfort zone may be painful for a while, but you will come to a new and larger comfort zone as you conquer the fear.[2]

My Terrifying Radio Career

I can see all of these truths applying to my own fear of speaking. After my "traumatic flop" as a collegiate panelist, I avoided public speaking as much as possible. After college, I went on to graduate school but eventually dropped that for "real" graduate school—being news editor on that small weekly paper, just outside Minneapolis. Part of my news editor duties (which included just about everything but setting the type) included calling in once a week to a Minneapolis radio station with a "live telephone report" from our suburban area.

At first, the prospect of making this weekly call kept me in a state of abject terror. I made the call from the privacy of my boss's office, with the door closed, and no one in the room but myself. How, then, could this be "public speaking" and why would I be so afraid? The power of the mind and the imagination is limitless. Every time I started to give the tidbits of local news from our lakeside neighborhood, I pictured thousands—millions!—of radio listeners carefully dissecting every syllable.

I distinctly remember making one report and almost succumbing to total panic. I simply could not get my breath. I'm still not sure how I managed to finish telling my vast radio audience about the latest fisherman to fall through the ice and what the city council had decided not to do—again.

Somehow I made that call each week and confronted that same choking, "I can't get my breath" fear of speaking to an audience. In this case, I couldn't even see the audience, but in a way that almost made it worse.

As the weeks went by, however, it became a little easier. There were days when I could read the whole report into the telephone without a hitch and still breathe normally! The butterflies were still zooming about in my stomach, but I did it, and I did feel better about myself. Eventually, the radio station decided to quit carrying "news from the suburbs," which I didn't mind at all. Still, I had taken some tiny steps of growth in public speaking, and I would take still more.

Love Conquers Fear

My next frontal assault on my fear of public speaking was teaching a class of junior high boys at my church. Here the audience was live, staring at me eyeball to eyeball every Sunday. I had no training to teach. They just handed me the quarterly and turned me loose. Of course, I could do it, the superintendent surmised. Anyone six-foot-two and over two hundred pounds should be able to handle a bunch of junior high kids.

Several of these junior high kids didn't need teaching, they needed spanking. At times, it was all I could do to refrain from forward passing them through the wall.

Many a Sunday I wanted to quit, but I wanted to grow even more. Teaching a bunch of hyper junior highs the Gospel of John was doing me a lot of good, if no one else. Every time I stepped into the classroom it was tough. Junior highs are like piranhas. They can smell fear and uncertainty. I had one weapon, however, that turned the tide. I really cared about those boys and let them know it by taking them on outings and visiting their homes. I doubt I taught them much from the Book of John, but I did become their friend while I conquered my old nemesis at the same time.

Since then, I've met a lot of people who fear speaking in front of a group. Sometimes these people are in a class I teach and I try to help them make some tiny steps toward growth by giving them nonthreatening opportunities to share. I try to help them say, "Why not?" instead of, "What if?"

Perhaps the best thing about it is that, while I'm helping them expand their comfort zone, I'm expanding mine. Everybody is working on growing in some area and conquering some fear. We're all just in different places on the continuum.

Say "Yes" to Fear and Conquer

One of the best ways to conquer fear of failure is to say yes to your fear instead of no. Instead of fighting back, resisting, and playing the victim, accept whatever it is you fear and cope with it. When you say, "Yes, I am afraid to speak," "Yes, I am afraid of this job interview," "Yes, I am afraid to confront my teenager," you are actually speaking from strength because then at least you have the option to do something about your fear and to work through it. But when you say, "No, I am not afraid," you are telling yourself a lie.

The "say yes" to life's problems technique is not surrendering to disappointment and failure. It means that you are willing to face it and turn it into success.

The "say yes" principle is sound, and biblical. Many of the psychological self-help techniques that are taught in secular books are useful—as far as they go. Their inherent weakness, however, is that they leave you relying totally on your own internal resources. There may be mention of "the spiritual aspect" of life and "getting in tune with your spiritual side," but the orientation is still within yourself. The foundational principle of the New Age Movement is that you have a little bit of God in you and all you have to do is find it.

The biblical position is much different. The Bible maintains that men and women are separated from God, but they can be reunited with Him through faith in Jesus Christ. And, indeed, when you place faith in Christ, God does enter your life in the Person of the Holy Spirit. Then you have every reason to be able to say yes to the most difficult of difficulties.

Saying, "Yes, I accept this and even thank God for it," means you can cope and triumph. To say, "No, this isn't right, it isn't fair, why me?" is to say no and be snarled in a knot of fear and failure.

Dr. Susan Jeffers believes the best way to face any kind of fear, failure, or disappointment is to choose to say yes instead of no. She suggests literally nodding your head yes to your circumstances, whatever life has dealt you.[3]

Most important, you have to be patient, not only with the situation or with the people who are making you a little crazy, but with yourself. You don't adopt a "yes attitude" to life overnight. It may take years before you learn to say yes—to the circumstances, to yourself, and to God. I heard of one man who developed the "say yes" attitude by remembering a favorite expression used by his aunt every time she faced a challenging situation: "It will do me a world of good."[4]

Thousands have been inspired by the way Viktor Frankl said yes to circumstances that destroyed millions of his fellow Jews during World War II. Sentenced to Auschwitz, Frankl knew the utter defeat and desolation of standing naked before prison guards who had stripped him of literally everything, even his wedding ring. Somehow Frankl survived years of starvation, torture, and abuse while his father, mother, brother, and wife died in the camps or were sent to gas ovens. Only he and his sister survived. The key to Frankl's survival was that he realized his captors could strip him of everything except his power to decide how he would react.

Frankl learned, perhaps for the first time, what Nietzsche really meant when he said, "He who has a 'why' to live for can bear almost any 'how.' " As Frankl tried to help his fellow prisoners, he took every opportunity to give them a "why" or an aim for their lives so they would have the strength to bear the terrible "how" of concentration camp life. But when a man lost hope and saw no sense in his life, no aim or purpose, he was soon lost. Frankl recalls that men would reject all encouraging arguments with the retort, "I have nothing to expect from life anymore." As Frankl says, "What sort of answer can one give to that?"[5]

The "say yes" attitude never quits expecting something from life. One reason failure is so terrifying for many people is that they make one mistake and label themselves losers for life. "I messed up once, I'll never be able to do it. I'm a loser" is an incredible lie many people tell themselves every day. The inevitable result is that they are immobilized—paralyzed by fear of what really is a memory, not necessarily a real threat or danger.

One failure can keep you trapped in fear of another one and around and around the vicious cycle can go. Also, fear of failure can keep you trapped in not being able to do your best, "choking," as the sports world puts it, and ensure more failure. But with the "say yes" approach, you learn to fail successfully.

Jill Learned Failure Is Never Final

In her fine book, *How to Follow the Shepherd When You're Being Pushed Around by the Sheep,* Jill Briscoe admits that when her husband, Stuart, took a large church in the Milwaukee suburbs, she had no idea of what it would mean to be a pastor's wife. Until then her entire career in Christian ministry had been with para-church organizations in Britain.

Quickly she learned that American parishioners had high expectations—much higher than her gifts or talents could achieve. Failure was inevitable and for a while Jill was too afraid of failing to face it. She even began wondering if God couldn't remove her from the scene, so He could get on with His work. "A bolt of lightning, perhaps, as I was hanging out the clothes?" she wondered in her lowest moments. She longed to be anywhere but center stage where she was stuck with stage fright every time she had to appear in public.

Stuart saved the day by telling her to have a go at it, even if she failed. "If the job's worth doing, it's worth doing badly," he quipped cheerfully.

"No, no," Jill muttered desperately, "you've got that all wrong. If a job's worth doing, it's worth doing *well*—and that's the problem. I can't do it well, so it's far better that I don't do it at all."

"Nonsense," Stuart replied. "It's better to do it badly than not do it at all!"

Searching through the Bible, Jill found a verse that seemed to encourage her to take Stuart's advice: "Whatsoever ye do, do it heartily, as to the Lord, and not unto men."[6]

Well, she thought, *I can at least fail forcefully*. So she began trying to do what people expected a pastor's wife to do and she did fail, and failed some more. But here and there she succeeded and eventually discovered gifts she didn't even know she had.[7]

Perhaps it sounds incongruous to talk about feeling guilty for feeling fear of any kind, including fear of failure. But if you take the Bible seriously, feeling guilty about fear is quite easy. Doesn't Scripture say that perfect love casts out fear?[8] And what about all those wonderful promises in the Psalms, such as: "The Lord is my light and my salvation—whom shall I fear? The Lord is the stronghold of my life—of whom shall I be afraid?"[9]

The answer bounces back from deep within our doubts: "Lots of things and plenty of people." And at that point the negative self-talk tapes roll and you start thinking: *If you really believed, you wouldn't be afraid. You don't have much faith. Some Christian you are!*

The only way out of this Catch-22 is through God's grace. Instead of wallowing in guilt and fear because you aren't measuring up to what a Christian "should" be, you can turn to God and ask Him to help you take small steps beyond your tiny little comfort zone. And as you take those steps you enlarge that comfort zone and conquer your fears.

God Is an "Eastern" Shepherd

Above all else, we must understand that we need not fear God. Revere Him, respect Him, and hold Him in highest awe, yes. But fear Him, no. There is no condemnation for God's sheep, no matter how stubborn, wayward, or timid they are. Jill Briscoe observes that across the world there are two basic kinds of shepherds of sheep. Western shepherds drive their sheep, Eastern shepherds lead them. God, says Jill, is definitely an Eastern shepherd. He guides gently and patiently, always ready to risk life and limb to retrieve one lost sheep, even though ninety-nine are safe. He uses His rod and staff to rescue and assist, not beat and punish.

The best way to handle failure is to know—*mark it down and never let it go*—that failure is forgivable. Perfect love *does* cast out fear.

Confronting your fear is a good way to see if your faith is maturing or still a remnant of long-lost Sunday school les-

sons that never took. The devil has no more potent tool
than fear and he uses our failures to make us think God is
far away and of little help. As Jill Briscoe observes, we
practice the devil's presence when we buy his lies and
then obediently repeat them over and over in fear-filled
self-talk. She writes: "I must learn not to practice the presence of my enemy, but rather to practice the presence of
my God."[10]

When you practice God's presence you say yes to whatever
life can throw at you. You say, "Yes, I'm afraid, but I'm going
ahead anyway." "Yes, I failed, but I'll get it next time." In
God's presence, failure is never final.

In Summary

1. Don't fear disappointment and failure; the difference
between failure and success is very small.

2. Guard your heart from burning ambition; instead, have
a drive for mastery but never be driven.

3. Never forget that failure and trials make you stronger for
even tougher times in the future.

4. Fear always blocks any steps toward growth or change.

5. The only way to deal with a fear is to go ahead and do or
face what you are afraid of.

6. Everyone is afraid—we all just fear different things.

7. Living with fear is more painful than facing it, fighting
it, and winning.

8. Your self-talk determines if you are practicing the presence of the enemy or the presence of God.

The following chart illustrates the difference between the
kind of talk that keeps you knotted in fear of failure and
simple countering language you can use to start unraveling
those knots.

Fear Talk	Positive Self-Talk	Practicing His Presence
I can't do it; I'm too scared—what if I foul it up?	I'm scared, but who isn't now and then? I've done tougher jobs—I'll try it!	"For God has not given us the spirit of fear, but of power and of love and of a sound mind" (2 Timothy 1:7 NKJV).
Talking to her is impossible; she is so intimidating, I never know what to say. She makes me feel like a fool.	She's difficult to deal with, but I'm going to try. I think I can get through to her.	"There is no fear in love; but perfect love casts out fear . . ." (1 John 4:18 NKJV).
I blew the whole deal—I'll be fired. I'm ruined.	The deal fell through, but it's not the end of the world. Next time I'll make it work.	"The Lord is on my side; I will not fear. What can man do to me?" (Psalms 118:6 NKJV).

The above examples are no magic wand. One positive remark won't miraculously drive away all your negative thoughts, which, unfortunately, keep coming back again and again. Just as with worry and anxiety, which are brother and sister knots to the knot of fear, you have to stop, think, and counter fear-talk with patience, courage, and faith.

The faith element—practicing His presence—is most important. You can try to do it alone, or you can use the Grace Factor, your most powerful weapon. Repeating, meditating on, and believing in God's Word will turn mere positive self-talk into thoughts that will release peace and assurance that is beyond understanding.

SEVEN

- ## Staying Out From Under the Gun

"I'd love to hit the links, but there is just no time this week," I tell a friend who's just called. "I've got to get this manuscript finished and I am really under the gun."

Have you ever used the "under the gun" expression yourself? I use it a lot, and I'm not sure where I heard it first. The origin of the expression "under the gun" is difficult to track down, but one story goes something like this:

In the days of wooden ships and iron men, a young ensign was assigned to oversee the shipment of a giant cannon from one fort to another. He personally supervised the securing of the cannon on the deck of the ship and all went well during the first few days of the voyage. But then the glass started to drop and the ensign heard the captain say, "Looks as if we're in for heavy weather. We'd better be sure everything is lashed down tight."

Naturally the ensign thought immediately of the huge cannon and went to check it. "I suppose it could stand another line or two," he mused. "But it's cold up here and I'd really like to get below to get a mug of the cook's broth and some dry clothes. I'll come back up later and put another line on it."

So he went below and had his mug of soup as well as a long conversation with the first mate about what the women were like in their port of call.

As the ensign downed the last of his soup, he heard a rumbling on deck and shouts of alarm that turned into screams of panic. In seconds he was topside to find the storm beating down in full fury and the huge cannon running loose on the deck! It had already smashed into the starboard rail and as the ship rolled with the waves it began reversing its direction to head straight for the main mast and two sailors who were desperately striking sail to better ride out the storm.

There was no time to think or even shout a warning. In one bound, the ensign threw himself under the wheels of the mighty gun and brought it to a halt just before it could smash into the two sailors and possibly take out the main mast as well.

As the ensign writhed in pain with two broken legs, the sailors secured the gun with extra heavy ropes and then rushed him below for first aid.

A few days later, the ensign was lying in sick bay when the first mate came in and said, "Captain wants you on deck immediately."

"What for?" he wanted to know. "It's not easy to move around with two broken legs."

"Not sure, something about the gun getting loose in the storm and your managing to stop it before it rolled right over someone."

With the help of two shipmates and some crutches, the ensign painfully made his way to the quarterdeck where he found the captain waiting with most of the crew.

Obviously, he wants to give me a commendation for my bravery, thought the ensign as he hobbled forward. He did his best to stand at attention as the captain read from a prepared proclamation that rehearsed the facts of the loose cannon incident and the ensign's brave act of self-sacrifice.

". . . In summary, this act of bravery would normally deserve the bestowing of our country's highest honors for heroism. Unfortunately, another regulation must prevail. For dire neglect of duty and negligence in carrying out your responsibilities which placed your shipmates in the most dire kind of peril and which threatened the security of the ship itself, you are to be held under guard until we reach port at which time you are to be remanded to the proper authorities for a court martial hearing."

Some versions of this story claim that the ensign was hung on the spot with no court martial even being held. Other accounts say he was given a medal for heroism and then sentenced to be shot immediately.

Whichever account is true, the moral is clear: Even the most heroic actions don't substitute for carrying out responsibilities promptly and thoroughly. Throwing yourself "under the gun" does not help if you are the one who let the gun get loose in the first place.

Another clear lesson is that procrastination never pays. The procrastinator is the one who pays eventually, sometimes a very high price.

Are We All "Born" Procrastinators?

Unfortunately, stories with morals are told and heard far more often than heeded. Down through the centuries, the human race has been warned, cajoled, and pleaded with to fulfill its responsibilities and not postpone what needs to be done. Nonetheless, procrastination remains one of the commonest of all sins of omission, which is often excused as "human nature" and accepted with a shrug of resignation.

In *Doing It Now*, his practical book on curing procrastination in twelve easy steps, Edwin C. Bliss defines procrastinating as "postponing something that you know in your heart should be done now instead of later." He believes that procrastination is the common denominator of people who fail to live up to their potential. In other words, procrastination short-circuits success. A successful person does not procrastinate.[1]

Some people try to claim they are "born procrastinators." They like to tell people they are "under the gun" because it makes them sound busy and important. I've played that game myself. I believe, however, that procrastination is just as much a knot as perfectionism and, in fact, perfectionists are often procrastinators. You would think the opposite would be true—that a perfectionist would efficiently get everything done right now and never put off any duty or responsibility. Instead, the perfectionist often bails out by way of procrastination and uses the excuse, "There isn't time to do it right so I won't get into that at all."

Because perfectionism is one of my biggest knots, I see procrastination as a perfect cop-out—at least for a while. Finally, sheer pressure usually causes me to produce. I have procrastinated for years and excused it by saying, "I work better under pressure," or, "I need a deadline to get motivated." But I'm finally learning it isn't worth it.

Another major reason for procrastinating is fear of failure, not being willing to take a risk. Procrastination is often disguised as "maintaining the status quo" and excused with familiar statements like: "We've done it this way for years." "Why fix what's working?"

Whatever has been done that way for years may not be working that well, but change involves risk and who needs that? It's much more tempting to keep things the way they are and keep putting off change and the risks that come with it.

A third explanation for procrastinating is plain and simple laziness. Among the seven deadly sins is sloth, which covers more than just being lazy. The slothful man ". . . loves nothing. He is a no-care, waving away existence with a gesture of the hand; he is the Bored."[2]

Proverbs 26:12–16 (NKJV) pictures the bored, slothful man who seems to love nothing:

> Do you see a man wise in his own eyes?
> There is more hope for a fool than for him.
> The slothful man says, "There is a lion in the road!
> A fierce lion is in the streets!"
> As a door turns on its hinges,
> So does the slothful turn on his bed.
> The slothful man buries his hand in the bowl;
> It wearies him to bring it back to his mouth.
> The sluggard is wiser in his own eyes
> Than seven men who can answer sensibly.

In the New Testament, Paul warns one church about sloth and says, ". . . If anyone will not work, neither shall he eat. For we hear that there are some who walk among you in a disorderly manner, not working at all, but are busybodies."[3]

Paul's words remind us that there are other ways to be lazy besides just lying about. A "busybody" is usually just that— very busy with matters that don't matter. Busybodies are great procrastinators, always talking about what they're going to do as they bustle about doing very little.

But What About My Overloaded "To Do" List?

"All very interesting," you might observe, "but I'm really not a sluggard, a sloth, or a busybody. My problem seems to lie in having just too many things to do and not being able to decide what to do first. I know I procrastinate but what can I do? What about situations where you have to put some things off because other things simply have to be done first?"

The Scriptures describe instances of legitimate delay or waiting until just the right time. When their brother, Lazarus, became mortally ill, Mary and Martha sent urgent word to their good Friend, Jesus of Nazareth, asking Him to come and help. Strangely, Jesus made no move to hurry to Lazarus's home in Bethany where He could have healed him in a moment. After delaying two days, He finally said to His disciples, "Let's go back to Judea."

Jesus could have rushed to Bethany and healed Lazarus, but He had another plan—another priority. Nature took its course while He delayed and when He finally arrived He prayed before Lazarus's tomb saying, "Father, I thank You that You have heard Me. I know that You always hear Me, but I said this for the benefit of the people standing here, that they may believe that You sent Me."

And with that He called Lazarus forth from the tomb, alive and well, still wrapped in strips of grave cloths.[4]

The story illustrates that some things can sound very urgent, but there is always the question of priorities. Jesus' greater priority than rushing to heal Lazarus from his illness was to show the watching world the glory of God with a far greater miracle.[5]

"Busyness" Is Our Red Badge of Courage

Priorities are the key to telling the difference between legitimate delay and procrastinating. Today, one of the best ways to cover up is to take on that familiar red badge of courage called Busyness. Everyone is busy. We all have too much to do, too many bases to cover, too many phone calls to make, too many phone calls to answer. What better way out than to procrastinate? In fact, it's expected. Ask a friend to check on something, ask an employee to cover, and the answer comes back, "Oh, I just haven't had time for that!" What the person means is, "I didn't want to make time for that because I have other things I'd rather do."

In *Strategy for Living,* Ed Dayton and Ted Engstrom observe that when we have more goals than we can handle, we need to sort out priorities. We can't do everything and even if we could, things wouldn't work out. Murphy is right. Things do go wrong, things are seldom the way they "should" be, and there is always a need to re-sort priorities, take stock, and regroup.

As Engstrom and Dayton point out, it is always "a question of trade-offs." And all priority questions are "when" questions. In other words, we must decide what we will do next and what we will do after that. The least important things may never be done.[6]

Is It Urgent or Is It Important?

The first priority question is: "Is it urgent or is it important?" When Charles Hummel penned his little booklet "The Tyranny of the Urgent," he observed that our problem goes much deeper than simply a "lack of time." As we look back on the year or the month, a pile of unfinished tasks depresses us. "We sense uneasily that we may have failed to do the important. The winds of other people's demands have driven us onto a reef of frustration."[7]

Hummel recalls the well-known prayer of confession repeated in many churches each Sunday: "We have left un-

done those things which we ought to have done; and
we have done those things which we ought not to have
done."

Seldom, however, do we link this prayer of confession to
sorting out the difference between urgent tasks and really
important ones.

There is natural and constant tension between the urgent and the important. Unfortunately, we don't always rec-
ognize that tension because important tasks are often the
kind we think we can put off. They really "don't need to
be done" today or even this week. Visits or letters to
friends, a careful study of important books, extra time in
prayer or Bible study—all these get nudged aside with excuses like "When I have more time . . ." or "I hope to
later. . . ." As Hummel says, "The urgent tasks call for
instant action—endless demands pressure (us) every hour
and day."[8]

As we put aside the important to do the urgent, we are
doomed to feeling guilty. We find ourselves saying,

"I should have studied for that test sooner."
"I should have planned the luncheon last week, not today."
"I should have gone to my son's Little League game instead of
another department meeting that ended like all the rest—no
decision."

Procrastinators wind up "shoulding" themselves, feeling
guilty, and promising to mend their ways—as soon as. . . .

"I'll start going to my son's games—as soon as things slow down
at work."
"I'll start planning things sooner—as soon as I'm assigned to
another luncheon."
"I'll reform studying habits—as soon as another semester gets
going."

And the procrastination beat goes on. Failing to do the important (tying down the cannon with extra ropes with the storm coming) leads to rushing around doing the urgent (throwing yourself under the gun). What can be done? And should we do it now or wait till later?

Quiz for Procrastinators

Maybe you don't need to take the following quiz. You're quite ready to own up to procrastinating too much. But in case you need convincing, try these questions.

1. When faced with big or important tasks, do I stall by reorganizing my desk, cleaning my cupboards, straightening files, going shopping?

2. Does change, risk, or a new situation cause me concern, even fear?

3. When faced with difficult or unpleasant situations, do I tend to get headaches or feel ill?

4. Do I try to get out of unpleasant tasks by delaying, criticizing, or complaining until someone else does it?

5. Do I make plans and to-do lists but have difficulty following through on them?

6. Am I staying in a job that I don't really like and find unfulfilling and unchallenging?

7. Do I put off tough jobs and wait for a "better time" instead of taking constructive steps toward solutions?

8. Do I put off dieting, quitting smoking, or that trip to the drug-treatment center by saying, "I'll quit when I'm ready"?

9. Do I put off those menial chores that I really want to get done but never do, like cleaning the garage, painting the lawn furniture, etc.?

10. Do I tend to avoid confrontations with friends, spouse, sales people?

11. Do I put off spending a special day or even a special few minutes with my children because I am "too busy"?

12. Do I use sleep or "being tired" as an excuse for putting things off?

13. Do I find myself being bored a great deal of the time?

14. Do I put off doing beneficial things for myself (i.e., an exercise program, a day alone, etc.) because I "live for my family"?

There is no scoring system for this quiz. If you find even a few yes's among your answers (and who wouldn't), procrastination is a knot of some kind for you. Procrastination creeps into our lives through different cracks. For example, your idea of what is urgent is different from mine or your friend Mary's. But quite likely, it is your "urgent" that keeps you procrastinating and putting off your "important."

Procrastination always boils down to priorities—or perhaps procrastination starts there. We put one thing ahead of another and before we can say, "I'm going to start next week," we are under the gun. But there is a better way to prioritize and plan your life, as we will see in chapter 8.

EIGHT

■ How to Prioritize Your Priorities

For most of us, it's not just a question of "having priorities." We all have priorities, but somehow they aren't in the right order. That's why we live in slavery to the urgent instead of living freely by getting the important things done at the right time. Learning to "prioritize our priorities" is the secret to loosening the procrastination knot.

To sort priorities, many time-management and life-strategy specialists suggest the "A-B-C" approach. That way you can assign each priority or goal with a value instead of a number.

A = "must do"—very high value.
B = "should do"—medium value.
C = "can do"—low value.

Suppose you have several A's. Simply categorize them as A-a, A-b, and so on. You can do the same with the B's and, if necessary, the C's, although, to be honest, you may seldom get to your C's.

Granted, you can still have problems focusing on your absolute "first" priority. Your A-b or A-c may switch around to suddenly become A-a. Don't let that frustrate you. What's important is to have a system and to keep working it all the time to keep focused on what you want to do next, what you want to do this afternoon, tomorrow, next Thursday, and so on.

Denis Waitley, behavioral psychologist and motivational specialist, uses his own version of the A-B-C system by keeping three priority lists on cards and in a notebook. His A's call for "action immediately," his B's for "action before the weekend," and his C's for "can wait." He uses color codes—red for urgent, yellow for this week, blue for this month, and green for "when there's time."

Putting All Our Books in the Nutshell

The key to any priority system is to keep the "urgent," "must do now," "action immediately" tasks from overwhelming the important tasks that need to be done but can be postponed. In my own case, I have several thousand books that need to be cataloged and put into our new word processing system called the "Nutshell." This is an important task because I'm constantly searching madly through bookshelves trying to find a certain book, which always seems to "move" from where I just know it should be. If I had all the books cataloged, this would save all kinds of time, not to mention a great deal of anxiety and frustration.

Unfortunately, cataloging books is an easy task to put off. It is not as "urgent" as getting the next chapter of this book written, not to mention the next and the next and the next. Cataloging books is not as urgent as writing two important business letters that have to go out this week. Nor is it as urgent as some very necessary errands that have come up today and must be run before 6:00 P.M.

How can I fight back and try to keep the urgent from shoving the important into the ditch? To get the book cataloging going, I have used several strategies that all focus on breaking the job down into doable steps or chewable bites, if you please.

First, I use the "salami technique," which is really an organized "to do" list that breaks the job into a chronological sequence. It looks like this:

1. Get all books gathered into den for shelving (no small task since my books were in boxes, cupboards, closets, etc.).
2. Decide on cataloging system (after much debate and deliberation, Jackie and I decided on shelving all books in alphabetical order by author. When we catalog the books with our Nutshell computer program, we will cross-reference each book by author, title, and subject(s), making it easy for me to look for a book if I can recall the title or subject, but can't remember the author).
3. Get all books on shelves in alphabetical order by author (I hired my daughter, Kimberly, to help with this momentous task).
4. Fritz goes through books and makes tape recording, cataloging each book by title and subject.
5. Jackie computes info into Nutshell program for permanent easy reference.
6. Go out to dinner as a reward.

We've already covered steps 1 through 3. I am now attacking step 4—cataloging each book by title and topic so Jackie can do step 5—putting it all in the Nutshell (no pun intended). Because it is still a huge undertaking, I resort to other strategies to "cut it all down to size." These techniques go by different names: The Five-Minute Plan, The Swiss Cheese Method, Dividing and Conquering. The idea is very old and very basic and, like many old and basic ideas, it works. I simply take a few minutes—five to fifteen at different times through the day when I break away from writing and do a few books. Armed with my portable tape recorder, I go through as many books as I can, dictating each author, title, and topic(s). As I get all of one letter on tape (for example, all the "A" authors), Jackie computes the info into the Nutshell program.

Granted, this is the slow, drop-by-drop approach, but at least it gets some of the books done. And, as I get some of the more urgent, important tasks completed, like writing the final chapters for this book, I can block out bigger chunks of time to catalog books. My goal is to get them all cataloged by the end of March.

This prioritizing business is interesting—and challenging. Can I make it? Since it is the final week of December as I describe my project, I am left with something like ninety days to reach my goal. Reaching that goal depends on another key step, actually it's a philosophy, in battling procrastination.

Action Today, Not Tomorrow

My friend, Denis Waitley, teaches two simple rhymes in his motivational seminars:

> *"If it's to be, it's up to me."*
> *"Stop stewing and start doing."*

Because I've had the privilege of working with Denis on several publishing projects, I've had opportunity to see him put these bits of doggerel into action. Denis likes to talk about being "pro-active"—and he has several techniques for hitting the pro-action trail.

First, he keeps reminding himself, "Action-TNT—Action Today, Not Tomorrow." He handles each piece of mail only once, blocks out specific times for initiating phone calls and calling people back.

When presented with problems or questions, he tries to give solution-oriented feedback such as, "What's your next step?" or, "How can I help you and what would you like to see happen?"

Denis tries to finish what he starts, and he concentrates a major portion of his energy and intensity on any current major project. (In other words, he sticks with certain "A" projects until they are finished.)

He does not allow himself to get sucked into group griping, pity parties, or grudge collecting. He concentrates on singling out people and things that can be praised and stresses being constructively helpful, rather than critical.

He limits his TV viewing to special shows that he has chosen with care, instead of just flipping on the tube to "see what's on." He watches news programs only on a "need to know" basis and doesn't put sensational "film at eleven" images into his head before going to sleep each night.

When he has a series of necessary, but unpleasant, projects, he lists them and puts a target date for completion after each one. Then he immediately goes to work on getting those projects under way. In some cases he may have to use the salami technique and work on a project a little at a time, but the major point is that taking immediate action on an unpleasant project reduces stress and tension. As Denis says, "It is very difficult to be active and depressed at the same time."

Another thing he has done throughout his life is seek out successful and capable people to talk to in person and to use as role models and mentors. He is a strong believer in "modeling"—looking at the lives of others, interviewing them, listening to their insights, and then using their wisdom himself.

Denis often says that *FEAR is* **F**alse **E**ducation **A**ppearing **R**eal and that *LUCK* is **L**aboring **U**nder **C**orrect **K**nowledge. "The more good information I have, the easier it is to make decisions," he told me. "Whenever I start a new project, I do my homework—reading, phone calls, listening to tapes, whatever it takes. It's the key to becoming pro-active."

Finally, Denis doesn't let problems get him down. He sees change as normal and whenever possible tries to view change as positive rather than negative.

The secret to making "Action Today, Not Tomorrow" work is going into action *right now*, not this afternoon or tonight after dinner. One of the biggest myths that keeps us locked into the rut of procrastination is the old Que Será, Será motto: "Whatever will be, will be." But to take motive-action is to say, "Whatever will be, won't be . . . If it's to be, it's up to me!"[1]

As Ted Engstrom and Ed Dayton point out, the best way to be pro-active is work at being an initiator, not a responder. Don't wait for things to happen to you or until you are forced to make a decision. Set your goals and go after them with Action-TNT. This usually gives you more options and alternatives, more ways to go. If you set good goals and initiate action to reach them, you will tend to make better decisions that reflect your best thinking, not hurried reactions or responses.[2]

And If You Slip Back Into the Rut?

Procrastination is like every other knot. It's one thing to decide to untie it or even loosen it; it's another to stick to it and get it done. An insidious force that will keep sucking you back into your procrastination rut is your feelings.

"If it feels good, do it" is the motto applied to anything we perceive as pleasure, fun, or enjoyment.

"If it looks as if it won't feel good, don't do it," is the countermotto we apply to responsibilities, routine tasks, getting up on cold mornings, duties—even obeying the law.

If there is any knot that thrives on feelings, it is procrastination. The procrastinator says, "I didn't feel like it, so I didn't do it." Because we live in a time and a society that emphasize feeling good, it follows that we tend to put things off to indulge ourselves.

You can look a long time, but you will not find Scripture or any other wisdom literature saying, "Just follow your feelings . . . be yourself!" My psychologist friend, Kevin Leman, often tells counselees and college audiences, to which he speaks on occasion: "Following feelings is a trap. What if we all just followed our feelings for thirty days? We'd wind up in jail!"

I don't know about you, but on some days I could wind up in jail in thirty minutes. As for my knots, following feelings only ties them tighter. In his excellent book, *How to Say "No" to a Stubborn Habit*, Erwin Lutzer observes that living by feelings can automatically develop into the sin of procrastination. Responsibilities surround us on every hand. There are calls to make, people to see, letters to write, the lawn to mow, children to comfort, fences to mend, dishwashers to fix—the list is endless.

You have set your goals; you have reprioritized your priorities, but you keep putting off what you know you should do. So, you start "shoulding" yourself—feeling overwhelmed, frustrated, inferior, and guilty. What happened to the glowing promises of "If it feels good, do it"? That imposter has removed its mask and is revealed to be a liar. "If it feels good, do it," is not the way to feel good at all. Precisely the opposite is true. Oh, there may be a quick fix, a temporary high, or an immediate rush of pleasure, but when it runs out, reality settles in.

Erwin Lutzer points out: "Shrugging off responsibility only increases guilt. The more you give in to your feelings, the worse you feel. Rather than satisfying your feelings, you actually irritate them!"[3]

You may have seen the following little story. Copies of it have been passed around for years:

> This is a story about four people named Everybody, Somebody, Anybody, and Nobody. There was an important job to be done, and Everybody was sure that Somebody would do it. Anybody could have done it, but Nobody did it. Somebody got angry about that because it was Everybody's job. Everybody thought Anybody could do it, but Nobody realized that Everybody wouldn't do it. It ended up that Everybody blamed Somebody and Nobody did what Anybody could have done.

The Lady Who Hated Doing Dishes

Procrastination doesn't have to be done wholesale to tie you up in its knots. Examples of this are as close as your own "to do" list. Usually, it's a few, maybe one or two, neglected responsibilities that do you in.

One lady wound up in the counselor's office because she just hated doing the dishes. She stacked breakfast dishes; she stacked lunch dishes; and she did them all at once with the dinner dishes. Granted, you or I might say, "What's the problem? Sounds like a good plan to me." But for this lady it was a knot. She felt she just couldn't cope with dirty dishes.

Instead of laughing at her, the therapist set up a program based on simple rewards and punishments. When she did the dishes right after each meal, it was duly recorded. When she did the dishes seven times in a row, she could go out and buy herself a modest treat. But if she failed to do the dishes, she was to punish herself by scrubbing the kitchen floor, something she absolutely abhorred.

After a couple of false starts and one serious setback when she stopped the positive reinforcement too soon, the lady was able to do her dishes promptly after each meal without the need of a "special prize."[4]

You may or may not agree with giving yourself rewards for doing the right thing. I see nothing wrong with it, as long as the reward doesn't become your real motivation for trying to change. The best reward for breaking any bad habit, like procrastination, is the feeling of satisfaction that comes when you "act as if" and get the job done right now.

Tips From an Expert Procrastinator

For me, procrastination is a sure ticket to a guilt trip. I know I've put off something I've had to do and now I'm farther behind than ever. And, procrastination will keep me feeling guilty until I determine to change my ways. Here are some steps that have worked for me:

1. Admit your feelings. Admit that you're feeling lazy, afraid, or too perfectionistic to move off Square One. Suppressing those feelings won't make them go away; instead, they only grow stronger. Scripture is full of honest people who admitted their feelings, including Jesus Himself.

Jesus was tempted in every way we are and felt every emotion we feel (except guilt), and He didn't hide His feelings. He was angry with the hypocrisy and lovelessness of the Pharisees.[5] A few days before His crucifixion, He made His triumphal entry into Jerusalem where He met with a crowd that included many unbelieving Jews. Jesus admitted, "Now my heart is troubled, and what shall I say? 'Father, save me from this hour'? No, it was for this very reason I came to this hour. Father, glorify Your Name!"[6]

2. Find encouragement, support, and reinforcement. Even Jesus had this in the form of the disciples, especially the inner circle of Peter, James, and John. On that last night before the Cross, He invited these three to accompany Him to Gethsemane. Their performance was lackluster (they fell asleep), but the point is, Jesus asked them for support during His hour of need. Don't hesitate to ask friends and fellow believers for their support when you need it.

My own support network includes members of my church who are part of our "Care Group" that meets several times a month for fellowship, Bible study, and prayer. Most important, however, is my wife, Jackie, who has modeled "do it now" behavior for thirty-five years and who has taught me more about loosening my knots of procrastination than anyone else.

3. Don't let failure separate you from God's love. *Nothing* can separate you from God's love.[7] All of the strategies, techniques, and plans in the universe can take you only so far. But then you will falter, and even fail. You will know feelings of guilt, fear, defeat, depression. In those moments you must be no harder on yourself than God is. You must fall back on His grace. He forgives you; can you forgive yourself?

I am not talking about ignoring sin with lame excuses or bargain hunting for cheap grace. But loosening and untying knots takes patience. If you can be as patient with yourself as God is, it will happen.

We may put off the important; God never does. God waits but He never procrastinates.

We may fail and our faith may falter. God never fails. He is always faithful because He cannot break His own promises. Keep Him at the center of your procrastination battle by repeatedly saying, "If it's to be, it's up to me—and Thee!"

In Summary

1. Remember—throwing yourself "under the gun" does not help if you are the one who let the gun get loose in the first place.

2. Procrastination is almost a universal sin of omission, caused by perfectionism, fear of failure, or laziness.

3. Priorities are the key to telling the difference between procrastination and legitimate delay.

4. The first priority question is, "Is it urgent or is it important?"

5. Prioritizing priorities is as easy (or as difficult) as A-B-C.

6. To battle procrastination, adapt the motto "Action Today, Not Tomorrow."

7. "If it feels good, do it" is a procrastination trap.

8. Be patient. If you fail to whip procrastination all at once, don't be any harder on yourself than God is. Adopt the motto, "If it's to be, it's up to me—and Thee!"

The following chart illustrates the difference between self-talk that can keep you under the gun from procrastinating and the kind of counterthinking that helps motivate you to do it now.

Procrastination Talk	Do It Now Self-Talk	Me and Thee
There isn't time to do a really good job —I'd better wait.	Time is short, but I can do a decent job if I get started now.	"Teach us to number our days aright, that we may gain a heart of wisdom" (Psalms 90:12 NIV).
I have so much to do—I don't know where to start. Might as well start tomorrow (or next week).	I've got a lot to do, so the first step is to prioritize. I have to start somewhere and I can always reset priorities if it's necessary.	"Be very careful, then, how you live—not as unwise but as wise, making the most of every opportunity . . ." (Ephesians 5:16, 17 NIV).
I'm just too tired. Better rest and tackle this later. What's on TV?	I'm tired, but I can take fifteen minutes to get this started. Action today, not tomorrow!	"The sluggard craves and gets nothing, but the desires of the diligent are fully satisfied" (Proverbs 13:4 NIV).

The above are simple examples of how to *STOP* your procrastination talk and *THINK* yourself into action. It may not always work, but when it does, you take another step toward less procrastinating and more effective living. The Scripture passages in column three are an ever-present reminder, "If it's to be, it's up to me—*and Thee!*"

NINE

▪ How to Commit Suicide—Perfectly

Everybody she knows wonders what makes Helen run so hard and so fast. An only child whose parents had been critical and demanding, Helen believed, "I only count when I'm perfect." At thirty-six, with three children, nine, seven, and five, Helen hadn't said no to anyone for years. At her church she taught Sunday school, Vacation Bible School, and sometimes subbed as leader of women's Bible study. She was also on the deaconess board, the worship committee, and missions committee.

But her "total" commitment at church is just for starters. She holds down a part-time secretarial job for a small realty firm, does ceramics (she has her own kiln), and plays taxi driver for her children who are in gymnastics, dance class, Little League, Bobby Sox Softball, and guitar lessons.

When Helen finally decided she needed to see a counselor, she was almost at the end of her energy. Her husband, Bill, came along and told the therapist that his wife was "always worrying . . . constantly running behind . . . always biting off more than she could chew, and always feeling like a failure, and sometimes even depressed."

Like most perfectionists, Helen keeps telling herself it's "all or nothing . . . if you're going to do a job, do it right . . . one more thing to do won't matter—especially if it's worthwhile. . . ."

Helen was made for the poem that says:

> *There's only one life*
> *Will soon be passed*
> *And only what's done*
> *For Christ will last.*

That bit of verse carries a powerful message that can spur many people into the kind of action they need to take. In Helen's case, it helped cover up her "Avis Complex"—trying harder and harder to be better than she really was.

A Dinner Conversation With Dr. Leman

Helen is a composite of many women who visit the offices of counselors like Dr. Kevin Leman on a regular basis. While I was working as an acquisition editor for a major publisher, I would often fly into Tucson, Arizona, to see Kevin about his next book project. On one such trip, I worked with him all day on a rough draft and then offered to buy dinner. He accepted and, unfortunately, also chose the place where we would eat. Kevin's idea of a feast is a jumbo burger and fries.

Pocketing an extra roll of antacids, I said, "Sure, why not?" During "dinner" our conversation switched to two of Kevin's favorite topics—birth order and perfectionism.

"Perfectionism," said Dr. Kevin Leman, as he took a huge bite out of his jumbo burger, "is slow suicide."

"That's quite profound," I replied, vowing that next time

I would insist on going to a place that served adult food. "As the notorious baby of your family who terrorized at least one of your high school teachers into retirement, you should live forever."

"But *you* may not," countered one of the country's best-known psychologists. "Your problem is that you are an only child—a discouraged perfectionist."

"What do you mean, discouraged perfectionist? It's taken Jackie over thirty years to teach me to hang up my clothes. I hate ties, and my lawn always needs mowing. And my desk—I have the messiest desk known to man. I have little piles on top of my big piles—"

"Nonetheless, you can almost always find what you want, right? All you have to do is go to the right pile, which may be under another pile, but you know where it is. When you need a resource or an illustration, you can put your finger on it."

"Well, I guess that's true—in fact, that's what Jackie always says. She can't figure out how I survive—"

"Of course I'm right," said Kevin, as he washed down his jumbo burger with half a glass of Coke. "I've watched you do your editing thing and you're very critical of manuscripts—very picky—a real flaw-picker, I always like to call it."

"Well, it's my job. It's what they pay me for—"

"Ah, but your real payoff is in perfecting the manuscript—getting it just right, turning each phrase until it's a golden brown."

The thought of something golden brown prompted Kevin to gobble down half a dozen French fries as I continued to protest my perfectionist label.

"Well, I suppose that's true, but that doesn't explain my messy desk or my overgrown lawn."

"Sure it does. You've learned—way back when you were a little kid—that you can't be perfect. There's always some mistake that gets through. So you work that out by being messy. You keep kidding me about my clean desk being the sign of a sick mind, but it's a cover-up for your own perfectionism."

"I'm still not convinced that just because someone is fussy about doing his job right, that makes him a perfectionist."

"Oh, I can tell you some other things that probably fit you to a tee."

"Such as?"

"It's a pretty good bet you start too many projects, which almost always guarantees you won't do them as well as you could have if you had decided to lay only one brick at a time instead of the whole wall."

"Okay, you score again. I always do have too many irons in the fire but I think we are mixing our metaphors."

"The other thing that gets discouraged perfectionists down is looking at the big picture—seeing everything that has to get done and then, instead of taking things one at a time, they just sort of chase their tail by procrastinating or muddling through."

"I thought you said perfectionists start too many things. That doesn't sound like procrastinating to me."

"Saying you're going to do something and even starting it is one thing, but finishing it is another. Perfectionists are known for starting things with a bang, but petering out with a whimper. They're really good at finding excuses why they ought to derail themselves from projects they're working on."

"Well, I do tend to start things and never finish them. But those are usually projects around the house. I might procrastinate a little at the beginning of a writing or editing job, but I usually close with a flourish and get it done."

"That's typical perfectionist behavior. They need some kind of deadline to force them to produce. Of course you finish your book projects. If you didn't, you'd be in big trouble. Not only your income, but your self-image depends on producing on your job."

"You're saying perfectionists have a self-esteem problem?"

"Yes, as a rule they do. That doesn't mean they necessarily have low self-esteem all the time, which you don't. But you do gain a lot of your esteem from being good at what you do, which is typical of the perfectionist. It's probably a result of a critical parent in your family. Remember, the little guy you once were you still are."

"Yes, I remember your thought-provoking gimmick—Which parent do you think of first?—and my answer is always my father who really gave us a hard time with his temper and critical attitude."

"Well, his negative influence on you was so strong that's why you think of him first. And that's probably why you think of the negative first in everything you do—you're a born critic—a born editor!"

"You've got me again. Jackie's always after me about being negative. I try to say I'm just being realistic, but she's right. I see the glass half empty, not half full."

"And this is what became your great flaw-picking ability. It works for you in your profession, which is quite typical. Editors, computer programmers, engineers—they're all flaw-pickers."

"So you think I'm committing slow suicide?"

"Well, in a way, I guess I do think you are doing just that. Your perfectionism makes you an all-or-nothing type—always pushing to do it all and do it right. It keeps you in a state of being off-balance—no wonder you're always complaining about being exhausted, behind, and overworked. Think about it."

Dr. Leman Had Me Cold

I *did* think about it. Was Kevin right? Was I, indeed, a discouraged perfectionist doomed to a life of futilely chasing the Holy Grail of Impeccable Flawlessness? He had mentioned my determination to "do it all and do it right." A little research proved he had me cold. I tend to be what they call a "dichotomous thinker"—seeing everything I do as either/or, all-or-nothing. I was made for the slogan that admonishes, "If it's worth doing, it's worth doing *well*."

Either/or thinking traps you into believing that what you're doing has to be terrific, ideal, or wonderful or you're a flop, mediocre, or a failure. There is no in-between, no position of "being good enough." Perfectionists think in black-and-white terms about their abilities and performance. There are no gray areas.

No wonder I often bite off more than I can chew. There is always more to be done, always another goal to reach, and never enough time to do it.

Goal setting is a good thing. In fact, it's indispensable if you want to get anything accomplished, but too much of a good thing turns good goals into bad ones. A good goal is just out of reach, challenging enough to be stimulating and significant enough to be gratifying when attained. An unrealistic goal, or setting too many goals at once, can put your target out of sight and insure frustration and failure or only partial success.

Wrong goals or too many goals set me up for what Kevin calls my tendency to get overwhelmed by the big picture. Some counselors call this "the hurdle effect."[1] The idea is that you look into the immediate future and see too much to do—all those roadblocks and hurdles up ahead. It doesn't matter if you've done similar jobs before. *This* time it's too much and you'll never make it.

Whenever I get overwhelmed by the big picture, I react in two basic ways. As Dr. Leman somehow seemed to know, I either back off or back out of what I've set out to do. Or I'll proceed to procrastinate, stall around, and finally muddle through, taking far longer to get something accomplished because the job is more of a burden than a stimulating challenge.

Feeling overwhelmed reinforces my tendency to be negative. As Kevin pointed out, I'm a flaw-picker—very critical and analytic. I like to excuse all this by calling it being realistic and objective, but it actually forms a negative approach to life that sees life as a problem to be solved and perfected rather than a solution to be enjoyed. This attitude is sometimes called "Maximizing and Minimizing"—meaning you maximize your failures and minimize your successes.[2]

For example, I may venture out on the links with my son, Jeff, and happen to hit a decent drive. He says, "Nice shot, Dad." I say, "Okay, I guess. Better than slicing it across the freeway."

Obviously, that's a good example of minimizing your success. On the other hand, if I hit a horrible slice, I'll tell myself, *There you go again, Ridenour. You can drive three hundred yards—two hundred of them forward and one hundred of them to the right.*

The M-and-M principle takes a terrible toll because it makes you think you can't live with anything but the exact microcenter of the bull's-eye. Instead of evaluating each performance and learning from your miscues or slight errors, you internalize them. Well-adjusted achievers rate their performance but perfectionists rate themselves and make everything they do "a barometer of personal worth."[3]

When your self-image and feelings of self-esteem depend on performing, even a good performance doesn't help raise your spirits much. It only keeps you even and you give yourself a begrudging, "It was okay, I guess—I should be able to do at least that well—it could have been better, of course. . . ."

And because it could be better, the perfectionist pursues to work out what is called "The Avis Complex"—always trying harder to be better, never satisfied with something that is good enough or even outstanding.

The following diagram pictures the endless cycle of frustration and exhaustion pursued by the perfectionist.

The Hopeless Pursuit of Perfection

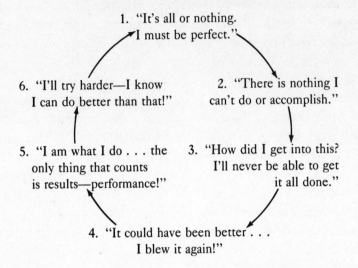

1. "It's all or nothing.
I must be perfect."

6. "I'll try harder—I know
I can do better than that!"

2. "There is nothing I
can't do or accomplish."

5. "I am what I do . . . the
only thing that counts
is results—performance!"

3. "How did I get into this?
I'll never be able to get
it all done."

4. "It could have been better . . .
I blew it again!"

1. Trapped in dichotomous-thinking, the perfectionist believes that life is an all-or-nothing, either/or proposition. The perfectionist has the highest expectations, nothing will suffice but flawless achievement.

2. The drive for perfection translates into setting unrealistic or impossible goals. The perfectionist bites off far more than any human being can chew by setting too many goals at once or setting his or her sights so high there is no possible chance to succeed.

3. Because of unrealistic expectations and unattainable goals, the perfectionist feels overwhelmed and suffers the "hurdle effect." Looking into the future, all the perfectionist can see are problems, hurdles, and obstacles. The perfectionist lives in the future wondering how he or she will manage to "get it all done this time."

4. As you hurdle through life, you confront the M-and-M principle, which means you maximize your failures and minimize your success and achievements. Even if you do well, it could have been better. And if you fail or even make minor errors, you kick yourself for not being up to standard.

5. When you don't meet your unrealistic goals or aren't even happy with goals you do reach, you feel inadequate as a person. Your self-esteem suffers and your self-image diminishes. You believe that your worth as a person depends on your performance and results.

6. You develop an "Avis Complex"—the compulsion to try harder to "be better next time." This only results in more all-or-nothing thinking, more unrealistic impossible goals, more feeling overwhelmed.

This diagram reveals the kind of self-talk that the perfectionist engages in almost constantly, as the perfectionism knot grows tighter and tighter.

Are You a Perfectionist?

Like most of life's knots, perfectionism is a matter of degree. You may have a severe case, or you may not be much of a perfectionist at all. Take the following quiz and see how you do. To compute your score, give yourself a 0 for "Never," a 1 for "Seldom," a 2 for "Often," and a 3 for "Always."

__ 1. Do you procrastinate because you think you don't have time to do a really good job?

__ 2. Do you see the glass half empty instead of half full?

__ 3. Do you find it hard to finish a project, and do you keep wanting to make it better?

__ 4. Do you get irritated when things go wrong?

__ 5. When working with a group, do you quickly size things up and start making suggestions, putting things in order, and controlling?

__ 6. Do you feel everyone should have high standards?

__ 7. Do you dislike the idea of being average?

__ 8. Do you "should" yourself a lot—that is, do you use the term "I should do this" or "I shouldn't do that"?

__ 9. Do you tend to get down on yourself if you fail or make a mistake?

__ 10. Do you think you are less of a person if you make a mistake?

If you scored 10 or less, perfectionism is not much of a burden for you. If your score ranged between 10 and 20, perfectionism is becoming a problem. And if you scored between 20 and 30, perfectionism is a major knot that you need to loosen fast. In general, the higher you scored the more you will battle guilt feelings much of the time. If there is a way to feel guilty, it's by being a perfectionist because, quite obviously, you expect too much of yourself, you demand too much of yourself, and you can't possibly meet those demands.

If you're quite sure you have perfectionist tendencies, try listing your priorities—the activities that occupy your time. Also estimate the amount of time each activity, interest, person, and so on takes. Be realistic and add 10 percent at least. Murphy was right when he said everything takes a lot longer than we think it does. After listing your priorities and the time involved, you're ready for the most important step.

How Helen Learned to Say "No"

It's easy to get activities, priorities, and goals all mixed up in a chaotic jumble that simply spells *t-o-o m-u-c-h*. Remember Helen, the super woman who cracked under the strain? Before she crumbled, Helen wouldn't have admitted she was a perfectionist. Why, she could list all kinds of things she doesn't do perfectly. But a perfectionist doesn't *do everything perfectly;* a perfectionist simply believes she or he "should" do everything perfectly—"do it all and do it right." Helen was doing far too much and a lot of it not very well. Once she recognized this, she scaled down her priorities and goals. The part-time job had to go and it was just as well. After taxes and necessary new clothes, she netted very little anyway.

And at church, Helen learned an important new word—*no*. Some counselors suggest being a bit selfish, which sounds all wrong to most of us, but there is a sanctified kind of "selfishness" that has nothing to do with self-centered greed and no concern for others. Sanctified selfishness actually centers on others and saving enough of yourself to be more effective in reaching out with love. Sanctified selfishness usually begins by saying "No, I simply can't take on the additional responsibility in the church nursery." Or perhaps, "No, I'm afraid I'm unavailable to help the United Way drive, but try me next year."

My friend Kevin Leman has a special word of encouragement to firstborns and only children, all of whom are usually perfectionists because they try to emulate the only role models they have while very young—their parents. His counseling reveals that many perfectionists are also "pleasers"—people who can't say no because they want and need the approval of others. So they say yes in order to please others and get that approval.

It's typical for a perfectionist to get trapped in a situation where she really wanted to say no but instead she said, "Yes, of course, I'd be happy to do it." Get trapped in very many of these situations and your frustration level will rise to the dangerous red zone.

As Leman points out: "If you can't learn to say no to people, you will never be able to say yes to life. There are just too many people who will take advantage and pull you in a dozen different directions to get what they want. Very often you will find these people in your very own family. But if you constantly find yourself unable to say no, it usually means saying yes to headaches and stomach problems."[4]

If you're serious about resetting goals and priorities and cutting back on a schedule that is too full, get out that word *no*, dust it off, and be prepared to use it.

Don't worry about becoming slothful and lazy if you start saying no a little more often. True, there are people who cop out on their responsibilities and fail to take advantage of opportunities, because they are lazy or prone to procrastination. Perfectionists, however, seldom have this problem. Most perfectionists need to work on being a little more average, doing a little less, taking on fewer things. If they can manage to cut back, it will make life easier for those around them.

Someone has said, perfectionists are people who take great pains with everything they do and give great pain to everyone they know. But perfectionists usually give the most pain to themselves, and sometimes it can result in total disaster, as we will see in the next chapter.

TEN

■ Pursuing Perfection Versus Seeking Excellence

Pursing perfection is not only frustrating and exhausting, it can devastate you emotionally and spiritually. God becomes the baleful Eye in the Sky, watching every move to see if it is done correctly and obediently. And when it isn't, guilt engulfs the perfectionist like a tidal wave sweeping over a Pacific atoll.

Dr. James Dobson relates a tragic story about a young man named Walt who started out with a fervent desire to serve God. But Walt's conscience was so sensitive he had personal standards that made the Ten Commandments look easy. He tried, for example, to pick up every bit of broken glass on the sidewalks or in the streets, lest a child might fall on it and be injured.

Walt's compulsive behavior extended into every nook and cranny of his life. He felt uncomfortable about enjoying any simple pleasure and also had guilt pangs when he bought something he needed or wanted. When natural sex urges welled up within, he felt even worse about his "sinful thoughts."

Walt developed an elaborate system for balancing each of his bad deeds with a good one, but soon fell woefully behind in the debit column. To be sure he would not forget his frequent errors and failures, he began writing them down during church, using the back of bulletins or visitor registration cards. Walt's pockets were soon overflowing with scraps of paper recording his ever-growing total of unatoned-for sins.

Finally, when it became obvious, even to Walt, that there was no way he could "stay even," he became spiritually confused and discouraged. God was just too hard a taskmaster, and to escape his constant feelings of guilt, Walt left the church and became an atheist. Totally misunderstanding the Christian Gospel of grace, Walt flogged himself so long and so hard with "unforgivable guilt," that he extinguished the last spark of faith and commitment that he had.[1]

Obviously, Walt was a perfectionist and then some. When he tried to keep track of his sins and atoning good deeds by writing notes to himself, those bits and pieces of paper soon became reminders of his all-or-nothing, either/or thinking. Walt set impossible goals for himself and was soon overwhelmed. He fell into a terrible state of M-and-M thinking, maximizing his failures and minimizing whatever success he might have in atoning for sins.

All of this took a horrible toll on his self-esteem and self-image as he was plunged ever deeper into failure and, of course, guilt because he thought he was out of favor with God. Walt had a giant Avis Complex as he tried harder and harder after each cycle of failure.

Finally, Walt simply ran out of gas. He did not understand that he could confess his sins to God, repent, and find mercy and forgiveness. He simply x'd God out of his life and proclaimed himself an atheist.

Did Walt's perfectionism disappear with his faith? Of course not. In reality, he simply substituted a new taskmaster (himself) for the One he thought he had been serving. Walt never did know the loving, forgiving, patient God embodied in the Person of Jesus and the teachings of the New Testament. He only knew a large version of his own perfectionist standards, a caricature that gave him no rest or peace.

Joseph Cooke Became "of No Use to God"

A similar story with a much happier ending is that of Joseph Cooke, a language professor at the University of Washington. His book *Free for the Taking* describes his struggle with perfectionistic legalism, which eventually led him to a nervous breakdown, and, finally, to new understandings of God's grace.

Cooke was born in a Christian home, nurtured in Christian schools, and enriched by Christian teachers and friends. He confessed Christ as Savior at an early age and believed he was growing year by year in Christian knowledge. Eventually, he received excellent training in a good Bible college and was commissioned as a missionary to Thailand, serving under a reputable Christian mission board.

Joseph Cooke, the young missionary, left for Thailand feeling life was wonderful. He was ready and looked forward to the challenges and rewards of a life lived in missionary service for his Lord. Three years later, Joseph Cooke returned from the mission field, a broken man. In his own words:

I had to return home to the United States with my tail between my legs, so to speak. All my hopes and aspirations were shattered; and all my skills that I had acquired through my years of preparation became unusable; for I soon found myself unable to preach, unable to teach, unable to read my Bible, unable to pray, unable to face the least spiritual challenge or duty without threat of personal disintegration. I was of no use to my God, to myself, to anyone. I had been reduced almost to absolute zero, and somehow I had to find a way to put the pieces back together, and learn to live all over again.[2]

Despite his training in the Scriptures, which included perfectly accurate head knowledge of the grace of God as spelled out in Paul's letters to the Romans and Galatians and many other places in Scripture, Joseph Cooke could find no peace nor satisfaction. He followed the perfectionist's pain-filled path to what almost became total destruction. He talked about "the grace of God" and "a God of grace," but the God he served was far different.

Cooke believed God's opinion of him was so low that he constantly lived under His frown and never His smile. All day long God seemed to nag him saying, "Why don't you spend more time in prayer? Why aren't you witnessing more often? What's the matter with your self-discipline? And those thoughts—why do you think those wicked thoughts?"

For Cooke, his service to the Lord was a constant regimen of "do this" and "don't do that." He had to yield, confess, and always try harder.

Cooke believed that deep down God considered him to be less than dirt. When he finally cracked, he was convinced that he could scarcely utter any word, have any feeling, think any thought, or make any decision that God really liked.

What's Wrong With Just a "Little" Perfectionism?

When my wife looked over the stories of Walt and Joseph Cooke, she said, "These are interesting, I guess, but—"

"But what?" I said, knowing full well a detailed description of "what" was coming.

"Well, I think you should define *perfectionism*," she said. "I interpret perfectionism as 'trying to be perfect beyond reason.' At the same time, if I'm having an operation, I want the surgeon to be a perfectionist. And when I fly up to see my sister in Seattle, I'd feel better if the pilot was trying to do his job as perfectly as possible."

"Okay, I see your point; maybe what we need is another word besides *perfection*. A lot of experts prefer to call it excellence."

"I like that. If I fix a dinner for guests, I want it to be excellent. I want the food to be tasty and attractively served and to have the colorful table setting say, 'You are special, we appreciate your eating with us.' "

"What I should do, then, is emphasize there is a real difference between seeking excellence and pursuing perfection."

"Yes, that would help me a great deal because I think there is a tremendous difference. I think I should always strive to do my best, which is seeking excellence, but I must be able to accept the fact that I do make mistakes and that perfection isn't attainable."

"What if people think that I'm suggesting they lower their standards?"

"I've had to alter a lot of my standards because of lack of time. For example, because of all my commitments there isn't time to clean the entire house every week. Things pile up, but when I do clean I do the best job I can. I don't think I'm a slave to perfectionism, but I'm trying to do my best within the circumstances. I'm seeking excellence, not pursuing perfection."

Jackie's point is well made (as usual). When choosing between excellence and perfection, excellence is certainly the better route to take, but how do you find it? How can you tell if you are futilely pursuing perfection or happily seeking excellence?

Walking the Fine Line of Excellence

According to David Stoop (*Living With a Perfectionist*), there is a fine line between happily seeking excellence and futilely pursuing perfection. As we saw above, the perfectionist is driven by an unhealthy desire to do everything perfectly. In this liberated age when women have become a fixture in the corporate scene, the message they hear all too often is, "If you really want to climb the ladder, you'd better do your job perfectly."

Studies show many working mothers harbor strong feelings of guilt as they are trying to play three incongruent roles perfectly—wife, mother, and career person. The guilt floods in when the woman feels one role is suffering because she has to give more attention to the others.

The seeker of excellence strives for quality and knows when a job is "good enough." The achiever who can say, "That's a good job—I'm happy with that," is far better off than the perfectionist who works tirelessly on something, going over and over the fine details and who is never satisfied or really finished.

In his book, *Balancing Life's Demands: A New Perspective on Priorities*, Grant Howard warns, ". . . the world is designed to extract every ounce of potential from us. We place similar demands within ourselves. Motivated by internal and external forces, we run to win, but we must be cautious. The legitimate desire for excellence could easily drive us to excess."[3]

One of the most powerful purveyors of perfectionist thinking is television, especially the commercials. One ad uses phrases like "When good enough isn't good enough . . ." and "When performance is a way of life . . ." to convince viewers they can't live without this product. Are these phrases from a pitch to buy a Mercedes or a Cadillac? No, the object for sale is underarm deodorant. To smell good enough isn't good enough. According to this commercial, one must smell "perfect."

To sort out the sometimes fine difference between seeking excellence and pursuing perfection, ask yourself these questions:

1. Am I striving to do my best, or be the best?
2. Do I tell myself *I will* or *I should?*
3. Am I motivated by a desire for success or a fear of failure?
4. Am I enjoying the process or am I focusing on the product, which must be perfect?
5. Am I setting a high standard to get the best for myself or am I trying to outdo everyone else?
6. Is life a challenge or is it a curse, crisis, or dogfight every day?
7. When I finish a job, do I feel accomplishment, acceptance, or fulfillment, or do I have a sense of disappointment, frustration, or even failure because it wasn't "as good as it could have been"?
8. Do I realize that nobody's perfect, or do I tell myself perfection is possible—especially mine?[4]

In all eight questions above, the seeker of excellence is described first, the frustrated perfectionist last. Ted W. Engstrom, president of World Vision, Inc., wrote a little book called *The Pursuit of Excellence,* in which he said: "I think we all take comfort in knowing that none of us will be judged on the *perfection index*. In the final analysis, the question to each of us will be: Did you make the most of your talents? Did you work toward developing your potential? Did you choose excellence, or did you coast? Did you rise above the commonplace, or did you survive on mediocrity?"[5]

It's that word *mediocrity* we perfectionists fear. The challenge is to go far enough with a project to pursue excellence, but never too far into the overkill of perfectionism. Remember, King Solomon said, "Whatever your hand finds to do, do it with all your might. . . ."[6] He didn't say, "Whatever you do, work yourself to death." As you walk the sometimes fine line between perfectionism and the pursuit of excellence, keep these truths in mind:

Perfectionism strains to reach impossible goals while excellence enjoys meeting high standards within reach.

Perfectionism values "what I do," while excellence values "who I am."

Perfectionism gets depressed and gives up while excellence accepts disappointment and keeps going.

Perfectionism is devastated by failure while excellence learns from failure.

Perfectionism remembers mistakes and dwells on them while excellence corrects mistakes and learns from them.

Perfectionism can settle for nothing less than Number One while excellence is happy with knowing, "I did my best, tried my hardest, and I am satisfied with the results."

Perfectionism hates criticism while excellence welcomes criticism.

Perfectionism has to win to maintain self-esteem while excellence can finish second or even lower and still have a good self-image.[7]

Grace or Guilt?

If anything can put you on a guilt trip, it's perfectionism. Your unrealistic expectations of yourself and others keep you feeling phony, worthless, angry, hypocritical, or bad because you can't measure up. How much more pleasant to enjoy God's grace—His unmerited favor and mercy. But the problem is, many of us say we believe in God's grace, but we really don't apply much of it to ourselves. Oh, yes, God may have "forgiven us our sins," but we can't forgive ourselves for our own miscues and failures.

That's exactly what Joseph Cooke, the perfectionist missionary, discovered. Cooke lasted three years on the field and came home broken and defeated. Why? Was the work too hard? No, it wasn't the work; it was Cooke's concept of God—sort of a cross between the Marquis de Sade and Simon Legree—that did him in.

In *Free for the Taking,* Cooke explains how he had to do some remedial study on the meaning of grace for his own life: He had to realize that when Jesus talked about being "perfect as our heavenly Father is perfect" (Matthew 5:48), He was referring not to impeccable, mistake-free, flawless living, but becoming complete, mature, and whole. Cooke knew that he had to deal with ". . . that attitude that makes perfection the prerequisite for acceptance. It is the attitude that says, in effect, 'I cannot accept myself if I in any way fall short of perfection.' And along with this attitude is the crippling conviction that other people will not accept me when I fall short. And behind all is the dreadful feeling that God will not approve."[8]

Cooke believed the perfectionist earns self-acceptance, as well as the acceptance of God or other people, by "being perfect." The perfectionist may claim to believe in grace, but he does not stand upon that ground. The perfectionist believes that God really doesn't love sinners but only perfected saints. For the perfectionist, "God is no longer gracious. The perfectionist is a legalist, pure and simple."[9]

As I work on my own knot of perfectionism, I concentrate on recognizing when I'm doing all-or-nothing thinking. Instead of lashing myself with "If a job's worth doing, it's worth doing well," I add *"well enough."*

I also work on getting rid of my Avis Complex. Instead of trying harder, I try *softer*, doing my best but not trying to play God and have everything under perfect control.

With Jackie's help, I keep reminding myself the glass is sometimes half full and many of my successes are well worth maximizing. Above all, I remind myself of Joseph Cooke's words about guilt, grace, and legalism. For me, God has never been the taskmaster or ogre that He was for Cooke before his breakdown; nonetheless I relate to how he felt.

Perfectionism, which is motivated by legalism, always leads to guilt. The pursuit of excellence, motivated by a desire to serve God out of love and gratitude, leads to blessing. To pursue excellence and blessing, take Jesus' advice and cast all your care upon Him, which will take it off yourself. The perfectionist's biggest problem is that he tries to carry his own load and Jesus has clearly said that those who are weary and burdened by their perfectionism should come to Him for rest. If you can learn to yoke up with Him and let Him pull the load with and for you, you will find the peace and fulfillment you seek. For His yoke is easy and His burden is light.[10]

In Summary

1. Test your tendency toward the destructive cycle of perfectionism with these questions:

- Am I an either/or or all-or-nothing thinker?
- Are my goals too many and too high? Am I programming myself for failure?

- Do I get overwhelmed by the big picture? Do I look into the future and see hurdles and obstacles?
- Do I do a lot of minimizing my successes and maximizing my failures? Do I see the glass half empty and am I down on myself a lot?
- Do these attacks of being overwhelmed and down on myself depress me and lower my self-esteem?
- Do I have an Avis Complex—do I always try harder to be perfect?

2. One of the best ways to battle perfectionism is to sort out your goals and priorities.

3. As you prioritize your priorities, get out that word *no*, dust it off, and use it more often.

4. Perfectionism can be a spiritual temptation and trap for the dedicated believer in God and can quickly turn into the quicksand of legalism.

5. There is a crucial difference between the unhealthy pursuit of perfection (never being satisfied) and pursuing excellence (striving for quality and knowing when a job is good enough).

6. For most perfectionists, God is more the stern taskmaster than the loving heavenly Father.

7. Use these tips to undo your knot of perfectionism:

- Learn to say "If a job's worth doing, it's worth doing *well enough.*"
- Instead of trying harder, try softer to do your best, not worrying about having everything under perfect control.
- A key to changing is to cast your care on Christ. Let Him help carry your load.

8. To make a definite commitment to dealing with perfectionism, take the following "Perfectionist's Pledge."

I am a perfectionist. Being perfect is very important to me. I may hide it by being messy in some areas, or I may flaunt it by being impeccable and fastidious. It doesn't matter what kind of perfectionist I am, my perfectionism has become a burden that is too heavy to carry. It keeps me tied in knots, afraid to take on things I know I'd like to do if I weren't afraid I couldn't do a perfect job. Here and now I want to commit myself to being more average, lightening my load of perfectionism by setting goals that are reachable and well within my talents and abilities.

(Signed)_____

ELEVEN

■ Why Guilt
Is the Gordian Knot

While talking with people about their knots, I have noted they seldom light up with sheer joy at the mention of the word *guilt*. It is not a popular subject, which can be illustrated by a fairly well-known story that takes place on a brisk fall day.

A man standing on a street corner in downtown Chicago points at a hurrying passerby and loudly proclaims one word: "GUILTY!" As the accused executive secretary or shopper hurries past while concealing startled alarm, the man resumes his stone-faced stance and soon points to another pedestrian and loudly utters that same word: "GUILTY!"

You would think that this kind of behavior would simply result in chuckles from the hurrying throng or perhaps a firm invitation from men in white coats to join them for a ride to a vine-covered clinic in the suburbs. Actually, the whole thing is a carefully conceived experiment, and researchers planted in the crowd can hear the accused persons muttering under their breath as they scurry on down the street. Are they complaining about "letting nuts run around loose"? On the contrary, the most common response by those who have seen the accusing finger and heard the ominous word *guilty!* is: "How did he *know?*"[1]

This supposedly true story makes an obvious point. Deep inside, we know we have something to hide and, understandably, we don't want to admit it or talk about it. As one husband/wife team who wrote a best-seller on guilt feelings said:

> It's difficult for most of us to talk about guilt because it's scary to reveal weaknesses, insecurities and human foolishness. We bottle up those feelings, believing that we're totally alone, probably crazy, certainly different. No one else has ever had these thoughts. No one else could understand. But it's not true. We're all there together.[2]

Not only is it "scary" to reveal our weaknesses, insecurities, and failures, but it's also embarrassing. Just about anything is more attractive than confessing our shortcomings and missing of the mark. Guilt is our Gordian knot—a metaphor sometimes used to refer to something complex, difficult, or unsolvable.

The original Gordian knot was confronted by Alexander the Great, one of the most powerful military commanders of all time. Young Alexander, who had assumed the throne of his father, Philip of Macedon, at the age of twenty, was fighting a major campaign in Asia Minor when he came to Gordium, the old capital of the Phrygian kings that was still an important center in the area. As the story goes, he was shown the chariot of the original king of the Phrygians and on the pole of the chariot was a knot that seemed to have no ends. Tradition held that the man who could undo the knot would be ruler over all Asia.

What happened next is uncertain and you can choose which solution you like best. Alexander, a serious, no-nonsense type, had no patience with puzzles and games. One version says that he simply drew his sword and slashed the knot with one blow. The other story, which one historian believes is "more in character," is that he simply removed the pin that held the pole on the chariot and then slipped the knot off the end of the pole.

It does not matter which story is true. The point is that Alexander untied the Gordian knot, which had defeated many others who had tried and failed. And he did, indeed, go on to become ruler of all Asia, or at least most of it.[3]

Guilt Feelings Are Everywhere

Few of us share Alexander's relish for campaigns and conquests. But we would like to undo our knots. Is it possible to slash through guilt feelings as easily as Alexander the Great slashed the Gordian knot? No, because guilt feelings are far more elusive. When I use the word *guilt*, I'm not talking about our objective guilt, which Webster defines as "the act or state of having done a wrong or committed an offense: culpability, legal or ethical." Nor do I mean theological guilt before God due to our sin, which Christ dealt with at the Cross.

I'm talking about subjective guilt—the painful, or at least uncomfortable, awareness of having done something wrong, having broken a rule or standard, having "blown it again." Dr. Bruce Narramore defines this kind of guilt as ". . . a complex cognitive-emotional reaction we experience over the disparity between who we are (or how we act) and who (or how) we think we ought to be. This reaction may involve self-punishment, self-rejection, and a sense of shame, disesteem, or inferiority."[4]

Or, in simpler terms, "Guilt is the 40 lashes you give yourself whenever you don't meet your own standards."[5]

Guilt feelings are everywhere. Psychologist Paul Tournier observes that we are all in flight continually. "Open your eyes," says Tournier, "and you will see . . . that huge crowd of wounded, distressed, crushed men and women, laden with secret guilts, real or false, definite or vague; even a sort of guilt at being alive, which is more common than we think."[6]

What Dr. Tournier and Paul Had in Common

You don't have to read very far into Tournier's books to see that he often deals with people who writhe in the throes of guilt. Tournier, a committed follower of Christ as well as a medical doctor, admits constantly wrestling with guilt feelings himself! But, then, he is in good company. Even a spiritual giant like the Apostle Paul struggled with guilt feelings. In his letter to the Romans, Paul said in effect: "I just don't understand myself. What I want to do I don't seem to be able to do. On the other hand, I wind up doing the things I hate and despise."[7]

Paul went on to determine that he saw some kind of "law" or "principle" at work within his soul. When he wanted to do good and right, evil was right there thwarting him. Paul concluded that he had two natures. His old nature was still susceptible to the power of sin. His new nature, which he possessed through the indwelling Holy Spirit of Christ, was in a constant war with the old nature.[8]

Paul seems to be saying he is something of a Jekyll and Hyde. He wants to do the right, but something deep within drives him to the wrong. And that produces feelings of guilt.

Why Do Women Feel So Guilty?

According to research done in the last twenty years, women can identify better with Paul than men. That's why leading women's magazines often run articles on guilt feelings and how to cope with them.

Writer Dianne Hales strikes a note with many women in an article she titles, "You've Done Your Best, Why Do You Still Feel Guilty?" There is the mother who leaves for work immersed in guilt after saying good-bye to the wailing two-year-old who must stay with the sitter. There is the dutiful grown daughter who travels two thousand miles annually to spend Christmas with parents she does not relate to or enjoy that much. She can't wait until it is time to catch her plane back, but would she ever miss the trip? Never! She would feel too guilty.

Hales observes that guilt seems to lie just below the surface of women's lives.

It nags, like a small, insistent voice whining within us, reminding us of all the promises we never kept and all the expectations we never met. We know that we're basically decent, well-meaning people, yet "the guilt" contradicts and confuses us. "You should have known better," it insists. "You should have done better. You should *be* better."[9]

What about men? Are they hounded by the same feelings of "needing to be better"? Studies show men tend to focus on specific acts like angry outbursts or getting a ticket. But in women, guilt is much more likely to be a vague and insidious presence, a disturbing sense of *being bad*. Psychotherapist Helen Block Lewis, who has spent two decades researching guilt, comments: "From childhood women care more about the opinions of others. They grow up wanting to please, to make friends, to be liked. Women crave approval and feel guilty when they don't live up to their standards."[10]

I've tested this premise while teaching study groups and workshops and find it to be true. Nearly 100 percent of the women present agreed that they are taught to feel responsible for others and that they are more concerned than men about the feelings of others. Nearly 70 percent of the women agreed that they have more trouble with guilt feelings than men do.

I talked to one mother with children aged five and seven and she defined *guilt* and *guilty feelings* this way: "God uses *guilt* as a means of pointing out our sinful nature. We are guilty as sinners, asking forgiveness in those *guilty* areas can then cleanse us from the sin and thus remove the *guilt feelings.*"

This mother seemed to have a tidy doctrinal definition for guilt, but when I asked her what or who makes her feel guilty, her need to please came out: "Saying no to the urgent commands of others . . . those overt, often accidental, words that pop out of my mouth that may hurt someone."

Another mother with children in their early teens defined guilt using the classic word *should.* She said: "The feeling that you did not or are not doing what you should be doing." When I asked her what made her feel guilty, she said, "When I don't handle problems or situations in my family the way I should. When I feel I am not living as a Christian should."

All this is not to say that men don't want to be liked and approved of, but their guilt feelings usually have a more objective origin. One father of teenagers told me guilt is, ". . . feeling bad, knowing you have done something wrong." What makes him feel guilty? "Myself, wrong action, not meeting my standards, not meeting God's standards."

When Enough Becomes Enough

Many counselors believe our culture has set a trap for women, and liberation really didn't make things that much better. Instead of being freed to be everything they always thought they wanted to be, women now carry a whole new set of "shoulds" and "oughts."

Carol Orsborn, founder of Super Women's Anonymous, remembers the day a young business reporter asked her what advice she had for women who wanted to experience the same kind of success that she had. They were sitting in her conference room at a table large enough for twelve, where Carol often conducted crowded staff meetings concerning clients who were a veritable "Who's Who" of law firms, consumer products, and hotels. Was she a "success"?

Before answering, she remembered a recent visit to her doctor. Through the Kleenex she had admitted that she was a woman who had everything, but still felt empty and overwhelmed. Part of the problem was a young son who had suddenly developed dust allergies and a baby daughter who had given her a royal case of postpartum depression.

Her doctor said, as only doctors can, "Your plate is too full. Learn to relax. Take some time for yourself. It's simply not worth it." She had taken his advice—sort of. She had gone out and purchased a microwave oven.

So, what was her advice to women? She took a deep breath and told the young reporter, "Enough is enough." In other words, enough with coping, balancing, and juggling. Enough with trying to have it all, enough with exhaustion and personal inadequacy. Enough *is* enough!

Carol Orsborn wound up on the front page of the publication the reporter worked for. And "Enough is enough" became the battle cry of Super Women's Anonymous, a loosely formed alliance of fed-up females which eventually spread around the world. She called Super Women's Anonymous "the self-help group designed for the woman of the 80's"— the woman already overburdened and overcommitted, who wants to make some radical changes.[11]

The secret of success that Carol Orsborn shares in her book *Enough Is Enough* is that the super woman of the eighties is already doing or feels she ought to be doing "at least one

piece too much." Five minutes of air force exercises aren't
enough. Jane Fonda pops up and lets you know you should be
able to handle a forty-five- to sixty-minute workout. And even
being able to handle Jane Fonda isn't enough. You should be
jogging. In fact, jogging was last month's prescription. *This*
month you should be pumping iron![12]

The "Shoulds" and "Oughts" Trap Us in Guilt

No wonder Carol Orsborn got fed up with being a super
woman. All those shoulds and oughts in her life helped her
realize: Enough *is* enough! If anything traps us into feelings of
guilt, it's realizing what we *should* have done or what we *ought*
to do and not seeming to be able to do it. Just what was Paul
talking about in that seventh chapter of Romans when he
said: ". . . I have the desire to do what is good, but I cannot
carry it out. For what I do is not the good I want to do; no, the
evil I do not want to do—this I keep on doing"?[13]

What prompted Paul's poignant admission of failure? Was
he overwhelmed by trying to be super missionary of the first
century? Had he taken a second look at a curvaceous young
maiden who passed him on the road? Or was he simply be-
wailing the fact that he hadn't had devotions that morning?

Whatever was bothering Paul, the furies of the shoulds and
oughts were definitely at work. It was as if he had discovered
a law or principle constantly working in his life. He didn't
mean the law of God. He delighted in that and wanted to
obey, but this other "Murphy's Law of Spiritual Ethics" kept
interfering.

Paul would have identified with the original Murphy's Law:
"Anything that can go wrong, will." There are all kinds of
adaptations of what Murphy supposedly said. For example:
"Two wrongs are only the beginning." And Paul would have
really agreed with, "Where there is a will, there is a won't."[14]

If anybody had the iron will to play the game "according to the rules," it was Paul. Born a Roman citizen of the purest Jewish stock and schooled as a Pharisee, he had a reputation for leaving no religious duty undone, no legal stone unturned. But here in Romans 7, Paul realizes that his pedigree and post-graduate degrees aren't enough. Even his Damascus Road conversion from bad guy to good guy doesn't seem to help. He knows what is right and he wants to play fairly and correctly, but the facts say he doesn't.

Paul Speaks for All of Us

The great apostle is not alone in his distress. We all have our standards, and we all fall short of reaching them. We are constantly aware that we have blown it—again.

Oh, we try to make the best of it. We smile and nod as we rub shoulders with all those seemingly guilt-free people who act as if they have it all together and even know where to find it. But in our candid, unguarded moments we mutter:

"I try to live right—why am I always slipping back? Why am I always feeling guilty?"

The answer is not in "positively thinking" yourself into new ways of acting. It is not saying, "I *can* do it. I *will* persevere. I will get on the ball and *stay* there!"

Nor is the solution simply "acting as if" you can always do the right and always avoid the wrong. That's just the problem. "Acting as if" doesn't always work. "Faking it" doesn't always make it.

So, what does? The answer is so simple it sounds like a cop-out cliché. As he hits absolute bottom, feeling as if he's tied to a "wretched body of death," Paul suddenly remembers something he seems to have overlooked. Like a drowning man grasping for a life preserver that has popped up in the towering waves, he practically shouts: "Thanks be to God—

through Jesus Christ our Lord! Because I have Him I can't be condemned!"[15]

Paul realizes that *by himself* he cannot conquer the principle or law of sin that works within his old human nature with such clocklike precision. Paul realizes that even though he fails, he is forgiven. He doesn't have to do time in "wretched man prison." He doesn't have to wear guilt like a smelly necktie.

When the guilt feelings come—and come they do—what he must remember is to trust in Christ's finished work. Then he can use guilt feelings instead of being abused by them. He can make guilt feelings springboards to further growth, rather than weights that send him on guilt trips of discouragement and depression.

Sounds great—for Paul. What about us? Does it untie any knots? Does it help us live up to our standards, or don't standards matter? Who has set the standards you live by? Your parents? Your spouse? Your children? Your friends? Society? God? And how can you tell God's genuine standards from the ones that leave you wallowing in false guilt? Just where does God really fit in?

TWELVE

■ Are Guilt Trips
Ever Necessary?

"Actually, I'm not that uncomfortable with guilt," said Reed, a young pastor friend of mine, as we exchanged notes on our most puzzling knots. "In fact, it's been an illuminating factor—a practical influence in my life."

"How so?" I wanted to know.

"Well, it makes me aware that God does have standards. For some reason I never have had a very tender conscience, even though I grew up in a strong evangelical home. You talk about the oughts and shoulds . . . it's true some people 'should themselves' for the wrong reasons, but that doesn't mean there aren't legitimate oughts and shoulds."

"For example?"

"Well, shouldn't Gary Hart have left Donna on the beach? Shouldn't Jimmy Bakker have stayed out of that hotel room with Jessica?"

"What I hear you saying is that there are eternal shoulds and oughts that mankind should obey—"

"Exactly. The trouble is, man hasn't obeyed God's shoulds

and that's why he's alienated from God. Fundamentally, all of us are fouled up. That's why we have so many knots in our lives. Would Adam and Eve have had any knots if they hadn't fallen? Would we? Our real problem is sin, which alienates us from God. That's why we struggle with standards, even when we know Christ has taken care of our alienation at the Cross."

We Can't Be "Religious Enough"

Reed's words ring true to my own experience. Over twenty years ago I wrote a book with the unlikely title *How to Be a Christian Without Being Religious*. It was a simple study of Paul's letter to the Romans, profuse with cartoons. The book became popular and reached far beyond its originally targeted youth market. Soon it was being studied by many adult groups because they, too, responded to the basic message which said:

You don't have to struggle on the religious treadmill. You don't have to reach up to find, please, and pacify God with "good works well done." You can simply be a Christian, saved by grace. God wants to be your Friend, not your Judge. He wants to help you become all that you can possibly be.[1]

I think *How to Be a Christian Without Being Religious* hit a chord, because deep inside we know we can't make it on our own. We know we can't "be religious enough." Religion might be great for "do-it-yourselfers" and the super-disciplined types, but it is a grim and rocky road for most of us. Religion keeps us feeling afraid, boxed in, phony, and guilty—tied in a big knot of self-effort.

So, does one chapter of Romans a day keep the guilt feelings away? That was my hope. I wrote *How to Be a Christian Without Being Religious* for myself as much as anyone. Alas, as true and appealing as Paul's message to the Romans is, guilt still hangs around the edges of life. Sometimes guilt winds up right in the center. Ironically, the same Gospel that frees me seems to turn upon me at times to bind me in the bonds of guilty feelings. Yes, I know I'm saved by grace. I know Christ has done it all. That's just the trouble. Because I know all this, I feel obligated. I want to live a life worthy of God's calling.[2]

I don't want to be a phony or a hypocrite. So, I am sometimes tempted to perform rather than to simply trust. The old do-it-yourself nature dies hard. Paul knew this better than anyone, and that's why he wrote, "Don't give the flesh (your natural human nature) a chance to get the upper hand over the Spirit."[3] When the flesh takes over, guilt feelings aren't far behind.

What makes us feel guilty? Ask any group this question and you'll quickly discover that guilt is a very subjective business. Some consciences are tender, others are tough. What causes you to cower in remorse and shame may not bother me at all—and vice versa. But what we can agree on is that in this life we never get rid of guilt feelings completely. Like the color of our eyes and the texture of our fingerprints, they are always there. Sometimes the feelings of guilt are valid and real, because God is calling to say, "Shape up!" But at other times, our guilt is false, or as some psychologists prefer, "unhealthy." Guilt can be a product of our imagination or our hang-ups. Guilt can also be a product of the hang-ups of our friends or authority figures who know how to manipulate us. And, sometimes, we can manipulate others.

"But We Drove So Far for Your Pineapples!"

It was the last day of our thirtieth wedding anniversary trip to Hawaii. Jackie and I were on Oahu and we noticed an ad for pineapples at an exceptionally good price. We decided to hop in our rental car and zip out into the countryside to see some tourist attractions. On the way back we would detour over to the pineapple stand to pick up some tasty mementos before our flight home that evening.

The pineapple stand proved to be more out of the way than we thought and by the time we got there, it was just past 5:00 P.M. I rushed up and found a couple of young men who were just getting ready to leave. In fact, they were officially closed for the night.

"You can't close now," I pleaded. "We saw your ad and we've driven all the way out here just to get some of your pineapples."

The two young Hawaiians looked at me—a hungry "howley" tourist—and then at each other with a knowing shrug of resignation. They disappeared and soon one of them came back with several pineapples. I made the purchase, thanked him profusely for being so understanding, and left.

As we headed back to town, I chuckled over how clever I'd been. Had I simply taken "We're closed!" for an answer, we would have driven several extra miles for nought. Since I couldn't let that happen, I had manipulated the two young men with a plea designed to put them on a bit of a guilt trip. I let them know that we had seen their ad and we had driven far and that they couldn't disappoint us! And it worked. We got our pineapples. Did I feel guilty for pressuring the two young men? Not really. After all, they were only delayed a few minutes and they got one more sale for the day.

Guilt Trips Often Begin at Home

When you think about it, we all put one another on guilt trips constantly in one way or another. Sometimes we criticize others because we feel guilty ourselves. And we often manipulate others to achieve our own ends, as I did the pineapple growers.

Sending invitations to guilt trips often begins at home. Are any of these familiar?

"What? You're not ready yet?"
"*Another* meeting? You're never home!"
"All the other kids get to. . . ."
"Why didn't you say something about this?"
"Look at Marge's husband . . . he works out a lot, I hear."
"Now look at what you've made me do!"
"We never go out anymore."
"John's wife really looks trim, don't you think?"
"If you *really* loved me, you would. . . ."

We send and receive similar messages on the job, with friends, even at church—perhaps especially at church.

The perfectionistic standards held up in some church circles put such narrow dimensions on what it means to be "godly" that it seems to make being a Christian and taking guilt trips synonymous. All manner of guilt provokers are spoken or written in the name of the Lord. For example:

"How can we spend so much time eating and partying when over half the world is starving to death at this very moment?"
"Why don't you witness more to your neighbors? What if they were killed tomorrow in an automobile accident?"
"Missed you at church . . . again."

And so it goes. If none of the above quite fits your experience, you can probably think of several guilt-trip inducers used in your particular group or denomination.

Even the Bible seems to put us on guilt trips! Paul Tournier writes: ". . . we fear the Bible, even though we love it, because it delves into our secret being as X-rays into our body."[4]

Is God the Ultimate Manipulator?

We have to admit Tournier is right. There is a certain
ambivalence in reading Hebrews 4:12. We are glad to know
the Word of God is powerful but we aren't always too
comfortable with how it judges the thoughts and intents
of our very hearts. Is God the ultimate Manipulator who
tries to put everyone under His thumb with guilt feelings?

A lot of people who come from authoritarian homes
and churches sing "Love Divine, All Loves Excelling,"
but they picture God as a stern, unloving taskmaster
whose stopwatch is always on them. Or, as we saw in
chapter 10, the knot of perfectionism may be causing us to
hold the stopwatch on ourselves and blame God for our
misery.

Guilt is often intertwined among our other knots. Perfectionism might just be the most potent guilt producer of them
all. Who can fall shorter of his or her standards than the
perfectionist who has set standards that are way too high in
the first place?

But there is also procrastination—and we often end in feeling guilty because we have put off something we know we
should have done.

Worry, fear, and anxiety can contribute to guilt. Anytime
negative self-talk kicks into gear, it ties us in knots that
eventually lead to the Gordian knot of guilt.

A husband worries about the bills and keeping his job and
winds up feeling guilty for not being able to provide ade-
quately for the family.

A mother scolds her child for bad behavior and warns:
"Wait till your father gets home and hears about this." The
child cowers in shame, guilt, and fear of what father might say
or do.

Guilt Trip or God's Voice?

The shoulds and oughts close in on us from every side and tie us in all kinds of knots. We could be spared many of these entanglements if we could only tell the real shoulds and oughts from unreasonable and even silly demands that we make on ourselves. How can we tell the false guilt from the real?

Psychiatrist Dwight Carlson differentiates by saying false guilt occurs when we hang on to beliefs that just aren't valid or true, while true guilt is the result of breaking God's absolute rules. Carlson often counsels people who keep telling themselves they are dumb, no good, ugly, inadequate, unpopular, and so on. Another favorite builder of false guilt is, "I have to be perfect." And as Carlson points out, when we violate any belief, true or false, we can have the feeling of guilt. Feelings of false guilt can be just as devastating as feelings of true guilt. Sometimes more so.[5]

Psychotherapist Archibald Hart counsels many people who have what he calls an "exaggerated guilt mechanism." Hart prefers to describe real guilt as "healthy" and false guilt as "unhealthy" or "neurotic." An example of neurotic guilt, says Hart, is feeling horribly guilty if you happen to step on an ant or some other insect. Unless you believe in reincarnation, this kind of guilt is unreasonable and irrational. How can anyone ever check every inch of a footpath to be sure there are no insects?

Hart believes neurotic guilt is far more prevalent than most of us would care to think and that it is based on violating "petty, internalized, irrational principles"—what Dwight Carlson would call "false beliefs." False or not, the results are still the same. They can have a powerful negative effect and rob us of freedom and happiness.[6]

Sue Found No Forgiveness at Home

Sadly enough, many of these false beliefs of our lack of goodness can come from encounters with our parents. A college coed we'll call Sue told me of a prodigal escapade she had taken part in as a teenager. It seems she got in with the wrong crowd and one night wound up attending a party when her parents thought she was at the movies. There was drinking at the party, which got rather loud. The police arrived and Sue (who had not been drinking) was picked up for breaking curfew while the rest of the group was charged with being drunk and disorderly.

When she got to the jail, Sue was strip-searched for drugs along with the rest of the girls. It was a humiliating and terrifying experience for a fifteen-year-old. Her father arrived around 4:00 A.M. and she was released, but that was just the start of the real trouble. Sue recalled:

> After that, Mom and Dad never quit using it against me, and to this day there are things I've done wrong that Mom will bring up. And the hardest part is that I wanted them to trust me and see that even if I made a mistake, I still had enough going for me that I could figure things out. If they could have just talked to me and let me discuss it and find out, "What happened?" I probably would have never gotten into trouble again. And when they would bring up my past, it would really hurt. In 1 Corinthians 13 it says that "love does not remember things that were done wrong," but it doesn't seem like that's what happens in so many families.

The sad final line of this story is that Sue came from a Christian home but she found no forgiveness there. Her parents kept imposing guilt feelings on her by digging up old bones that should have been buried and left there.

Archibald Hart believes that one reason why too many church members become victimized by neurotic guilt is that they have an inadequate concept of God, sin, and forgiveness. "Forgiveness is the genius of Christianity," he says. "No other religious belief system places it as central as the Gospel does. What else is the Cross about? God knew when He created us that we would need forgiveness. It is for *our* benefit."[7]

Guilt Trips Versus Godly Sorrow

Dr. Bruce Narramore draws an even finer line between true and false guilt and prefers to use the terms "psychological guilt" and "constructive godly sorrow." Narramore links psychological guilt to feelings of shame, fear, and loss of self-esteem: "Sometimes fear and guilt are so closely tied together that it is difficult to tell the difference. If we feel inwardly guilty, we expect others to punish or condemn us. And fearing punishment, we learn to punish ourselves much like a child spanks his own hand when his mother catches him in the cookie jar!"[8]

According to Narramore, the antithesis to false psychological guilt is genuine guilt or what he likes to call constructive godly sorrow. "The key difference between psychological guilt and constructive sorrow," says Narramore, "is that psychological guilt is a self-punitive process and constructive sorrow is a love-motivated desire to change that is rooted in concern for others. I believe a confusion of psychological guilt and constructive sorrow has often interfered with the church's efforts in promoting wholeness and health in the body of Christ."[9]

Narramore believes that feelings of psychological or false guilt are "always a product of our early family training." We think, *You fouled it up, you did something wrong. You're bad. What a hypocrite you are.*

A tragic example of the power of false guilt is this brief suicide note. It is full of misspellings that are typical of the ten-year-olds who wrote it:

Dear Mom and Dad:
   We committed sueaside because wear no good and no longer a part of the family. So, solong from us. Rembrance. Sorry about this.

Later, the mother of the twin ten-year-old brothers returned home to find one of her sons with a knife protruding from a self-inflicted wound in the abdomen. Both boys had also taken rat poison and inhaled ether from an aerosol can used to start cars in cold weather. Why had the twins done it? Because of remorse they felt for being severely scolded by their father who had ordered them to write "Stealing and lying are two commandments that should not be broken" six hundred times.

Twins "to the end" they tried to do everything together— even die of remorse for what they thought were "unforgivable sins." Fortunately, both boys survived their suicide attempt, which was triggered by the power of young and tender consciences that put them on a guilt trip that was nearly fatal.[10]

When your conscience waves a red flag, how can you tell the difference between a guilt trip, which is nonproductive and harmful, and "true guilt," or what Dr. Bruce Narramore prefers to call "constructive godly sorrow"?

Narramore refers to 2 Corinthians 7:10: "Godly sorrow brings repentance that leads to salvation and leaves no regret, but worldly sorrow brings death" (NIV). Paul is telling the Corinthians there is a big difference between feeling "worldly sorrow," which separates you from God's grace, and "godly sorrow" that centers on true repentance and willingness to change behavior.

In an earlier letter he wrote to the Corinthians, Paul had to correct and reprove them for many problems and offenses. He knows that letter made them sorrowful, but he can see that it was a godly sorrow because their actions have proved their willingness to change their ways instead of just wallowing in a guilt trip. As Paul goes on to say: "See what this godly sorrow has produced in you: what earnestness, what eagerness to clear yourselves, what indignation, what alarm, what longing, what concern, what readiness to see justice done . . ." (2 Corinthians 7:11 NIV).

Godly Sorrow Focuses on Others

Bruce Narramore believes that psychological guilt and constructive sorrow are very different feelings. Psychological guilt—the guilt trip—is largely self-centered, focusing on "Oh, what a failure I am" or "What will everyone think?" or "I'm just no good, I'm a loser." This kind of guilt focuses on the past and failures of the past.

Constructive godly sorrow, on the other hand, focuses more on others—God or members of our family, friends, acquaintances. Godly sorrow produces a concern, not about failures of the past, but what can be done right now or in the future to make amends.

To sum up, psychological guilt usually finds me focusing on myself and my past misdeeds. I'm motivated only by a desire to avoid feeling bad. I may feel angry and frustrated, which leads to a lower self-image and less self-esteem. Above all, psychological guilt results in surface change at best, or in no change at all, because I have the wrong attitude, which is really a combination of rebellion, apathy, or hopelessness.

Constructive godly sorrow focuses on God and others and the damage that has been done and what I can do about it. I'm motivated by desire to make things right, to help others, and grow myself as I do God's will. Instead of feelings of anger and frustration, I have feelings of self-respect and rightful concern and my self-image does not go down but rises with my self-esteem. The final result is that I repent—I truly regret what I've done and want a real change in my behavior. My attitudes are not rebellious or apathetic, but instead center on love, respect for others, and self-respect.[11]

To see how all this works, suppose, for example, I am in the midst of writing, and I am interrupted by my grandchildren, Matt, Chelsie, and Landon, who sometimes drop in without much warning. I snap at them and make them feel bad. I feel guilty for getting angry and face a choice. I can take a guilt trip and sulk as I play the part of the "wounded writer" whose creativity has been violated. I can let them all know they are the cause of my bad temper and it's "all their fault."

On the other hand, I know I've been wrong to be so impatient and I'm in the doghouse with everybody. Instead of feeling self-pity, I can decide to pursue real repentance for my ill humor. I can show constructive godly sorrow and go to my grandchildren, tell them I'm really sorry for snapping at them, and ask them to forgive me. I am motivated not by self-pity but by the desire to make things right with the loved ones whom I have offended.

The difference between taking a guilt trip and pursuing constructive godly sorrow is in that word *repent*. To repent is to go beyond regret or even remorse. The Greek word used in the New Testament means to "change one's mind." Real repentance demonstrates a changed mind that leads to a changed behavior, which is easier vowed than done. If you're like me, you've repented of sins and vowed to change but have found it slow going.

In other words, I can repent and ask forgiveness of my grandchildren but there will inevitably be another day when I lose patience with them again. In fact, there are some days when it seems like one step forward and three back. Sometimes it seems as if I lose more rounds than I win, failing to be all that God wants me to be. What I must remember is that Jesus didn't say ". . . be perfect all at once." When He said, "Be perfect . . . as your Father in heaven is perfect,"[12] He meant grow up, mature, become complete. As the Apostle Peter put it, ". . . grow in the grace and knowledge of our Lord and Savior Jesus Christ. . . ."[13]

And that is always our final question. To grow in grace—how is it done?

In Summary

1. Don't shrink from admitting guilt. Guilt feelings are everywhere. Everyone is laden with secret guilts, real or false, definite or vague. Guilt can be your friend as well as your enemy.

2. Even the Apostle Paul, writer of much of the New Testament, struggled with feelings of guilt. He knew how it felt to not do the right thing and keep doing what he knew was wrong.

3. Women wrestle with guilt feelings more than men because society trains them to feel guilty. They are conditioned to think, "You should have done better, you should *be* better."

4. We cause many of our guilt feelings by "shoulding ourselves" with unreasonable or unrealistic demands or expectations.

5. Our neurotic "shoulds" and "oughts" are not to be confused with God's eternal shoulds. The former produce false guilt, the latter, genuine guilt that must be dealt with through His grace.

6. False guilt is based on violating petty, internalized, irrationalized principles—false beliefs. Though false, this kind of guilt can be as painful as real guilt—sometimes more so.

7. Genuine guilt causes constructive godly sorrow and the desire to change.

8. False guilt is usually self-centered and asks, "What will people think? I'm no good—I have failed." Constructive godly sorrow focuses on concern for God and others and asks, "What can I do about this?"

9. To tell the difference between a false guilt trip and God's voice beckoning you to constructive sorrow, ask these questions when you feel guilty:

  a. Is it clearly forbidden by Scripture?
  b. Is it clearly affecting my relationship to God?
  c. On whom am I focusing, myself and how I feel, or on God and others, their feelings or welfare?
  d. What is my basic attitude? Am I angry, frustrated, fearful, resentful, or rebellious? Or am I truly sorrowful, concerned, repentant, and eager to set things straight?
  e. Is there anything I can do about this? Apologize? Ask forgiveness? Make restitution? Change behavior? Or is there really nothing I can do? If there is nothing I can do, I must leave the matter in God's hands and rely on His promises of peace (John 14:27, Philippians 4:6, 7).

A dramatic example of constructive godly sorrow is this true, first-person account by a flight attendant. She shared her account in "Flight Pattern," a newsletter published by the Airport Chaplaincy, which ministers to travelers and airline personnel out of Sea-Tac International Airport in Seattle, Washington:

> No one knew I had lied about my age on the airline application form except God and my friend, Margaret.* It was a well kept secret nobody ever needed to know. Yet, God would not let me forget.

* Names have been changed to protect privacy.

I didn't think it was a big deal at the time. I had lied before to get a job as a dishwasher. It was only part of that survival of the fittest philosophy where a person looks out for himself. Others lied about their age. Why shouldn't I?

Then, one day I invited Jesus Christ into my life as Lord and Saviour. God knew I had lied—and that made the difference.

"But it's such an insignificant sin," I pleaded in my defense. "Why can't I just pretend it never happened?" Eventually, I understood that Jesus Christ had died at Calvary for those "insignificant lies" of mine.

I could not possibly get right with God or witness to my friend Margaret without bringing the matter into the open. I knew what I had to do, consequences notwithstanding. I made an appointment to see the manager of the flight attendants.

I was willing to risk my job to be right with God. It wasn't easy, for I truly liked my work.

I got the jitters before the interview, especially as I had to wait for two and one-half hours. I had the chance to back away. Instead, I prayed: "You gave me this job, LORD. You can take it away if You wish. Not my will—but Yours."

"Are you okay?" the manager asked as I stepped into her office. "What's this all about?"

"I lied about my age when I came to work with the Company," I began, my voice quivering. "There are several people on the seniority list who should be above me."

"Why do you feel compelled to tell me this?" the manager questioned, confused as to my motives.

"I accepted Jesus Christ as my Saviour two years ago," I replied, "and this matter has been a hindrance in my relationship with Him. I cannot draw nearer to Jesus until this affair is settled."

"This has never happened before," my boss commented. "Are you aware that you could lose your job?"

"Yes," I answered. "I want you to do what is right for the Company and those other employees on the seniority list. I fully expect to lose my job. If you have to fire me, I certainly understand." Amazingly, we then prayed together that God would help her make the right decision.

When I walked out of the office, it was as if a ton of bricks had been lifted off my shoulders. Even though I might lose my job, I had the peace of God which passeth all understanding. I had no fear for the future. God would not forsake me.

Later that day, I received a phone call saying that the Company had decided to not fire me. The seniority list was to be adjusted accordingly. Yet, the affair was not finished.

I learned that a fellow worker had been laid off for four months because she was lower than I on the seniority list. If I had not lied about my age, I would have been laid off instead of her. As a consequence, she had lost four months of salary amounting to a few thousand dollars.

"I need to make some kind of compensation to you," I suggested to the one I had wronged. "I do have two years' sick leave and holiday which you could have." She agreed—but the Company didn't.

"You'll have to take care of this on your own," they declared.

So, regularly each month, over a period of two years, I repaid what I owed her. There was a joy in my heart every time I remitted the money. I was at peace with God and that mattered above everything else.[14]

THIRTEEN

▪ The Bridge Over Performance Gap

In *Free for the Taking*, Joseph Cooke describes his long, hard pilgrimage back from the despair and depression that brought him home from the mission field a ruined, broken man. As a missionary, he compared the Law of God to himself and saw a huge performance gap. To cope, Cooke practiced various forms of legalism and gritting his teeth as he "tried harder." When this didn't work, he said, "Forget it," and shifted to the other extreme of lowering God's standards or just ignoring them.[1]

Neither approach worked because legalism only made Cooke feel more miserable, as God seemed to point His demanding finger more often than ever. Trying to "forget it" and ignore the Law's requirements made Cooke feel even more alienated from the Lord he so desperately wanted to please.

Joseph Cooke's dilemma is a familiar one. Legalists turn their faith into a set of do's and don'ts they believe they can keep and futilely try to convince themselves that they are

living up to what God expects. At the other extreme, antino-
mians claim they are free from all restraints of the law and
wind up somewhere between playing lukewarm religious
games and licentiousness. The antinomian (lawless) approach
is a favorite among some dispensers of popular secular psychology. The key, they claim, is to stop "shoulding yourself"
with all those old-fashioned hang-ups. Ignore your guilt or
retrain your conscience according to modern, up-to-date standards that help you find self-fulfillment. One writer calls this
the "Mae West Theory of Personal Morality" because it fits so
perfectly with one of West's well-known quips: "To err is
human, but it feels divine."[2]

The Mae West approach is tempting. While we may not be
so crass as to err in order to feel divine, we at least want to feel
a little more comfortable about our many errors. When the
performance gap becomes painfully evident, why be a Phar-
isaical hypocrite, trying to kid yourself into thinking you are
better than you really are? Since there is no living with God's
"impossible to keep" laws, why emphasize them? After all,
aren't we under grace, not Law? A God of love, blessing, and
good feelings is far more attractive than a hard-nosed, legalistic tyrant who rains constantly on everyone's parade.

Millions Seem to Prefer "Cheap Grace"

Over the last few decades, millions of Christians have been
influenced by the "God is all love and graciousness" approach. God *is* love and He *is* gracious, but to paraphrase a
question Paul once asked, "Should we slip and slide into sin
because we know grace is so plentiful?"[3]

In *Hot Tub Religion*, his laser-accurate assessment of Christianity in our time, theologian J. I. Packer chooses the hot tub
as the most fitting symbol of contemporary Western culture.
In the West we work overtime at finding pleasant ways to

relax, have fun, *and enjoy*. Unfortunately, much of the Christian church is better at reflecting culture than reforming it. Packer observes that the pleasure-seeking syndrome (hedonism) ". . . bends holiness out of shape, and hedonism today has a very tight hold on our priorities."[4]

Another name for hot tub religion is what Dietrich Bonhoeffer so aptly labeled "cheap grace." To Bonhoeffer, cheap grace meant the kind that could be sold in the religious marketplace by the church itself with no questions asked or no limits fixed. It was grace without price and grace without cost—just go through the religious motions.

"Cheap grace," wrote Bonhoeffer, "is the grace we bestow on ourselves. Cheap grace is the preaching of forgiveness without requiring repentance . . . cheap grace is grace without discipleship, grace without the cross, grace without Jesus Christ, living and incarnate."[5]

As we all discover, sooner or later, cheap grace never really works or never really lasts. We may try to enamel our consciences with a rose-colored gospel, but we continue to feel the knots of dis-ease grow ever tighter, because deep down we know John 3:16 isn't talking about something cheap.

What do we mean, then, when we speak of the grace of God? To speak of cheap grace implies there is a costly grace. Is costly grace the kind we want? According to Bonhoeffer, costly grace is Christ's kingly rule, that treasure hidden in the field, that pearl of great price. This kind of grace is costly because it demands something from us—to follow Jesus Christ, not our own instincts, appetites, and ambitions.[6] It is through costly grace that we can and will untie our knots.

The standard definition of *grace* is "God's unmerited favor and mercy." That's a good start, but only the beginning of an adequate description.

As Larry Richards points out in *The Expository Dictionary of Bible Words*, *grace* is a word that expresses a radical view of life related to God. Grace, says Richards, is no tyrant or police-man. Grace means He accepts and loves us—as is—with all our sins, needs, and knots and we can approach Him with confidence, not craven fear.[7]

Costly grace proclaims that God acted in and through Jesus Christ to rescue all of us from a universal predicament.[8] Costly grace recognizes that every human being is hopelessly trapped in sin with no ability to please God or gain His approval.[9] Through costly grace, He comes to the aid of anyone who trusts Christ, and not his own good works, for salvation.[10]

Richards writes: "Grace is a way of life. Relying totally on Jesus to work within us, we experience God's own unlimited power, vitalizing us and enabling us to live truly good lives."[11]

The most amazing thing about costly grace is that it's free—as Joseph Cooke puts it—free for the taking. Grace is God's gift of faith given to us at ultimate cost to Him.

Note, however, the recipients of grace are always those who are weak enough and humble enough to take what God offers. Grace always reaches out a hand to help—not with a bribe, a reward, or even a handout—but with a gift of unconditional love, delivered with no quid pro quo strings attached.

Paul Had to Grow in Grace, Too

As a young man, Saul the Pharisee knew nothing of grace. He knew all there was to know about law and obtaining righteousness through self-effort.

But Saul changed; more correctly, he was changed in a blinding encounter with Christ on the road to Damascus.[12] Saul became Paul, the great Christian apostle of grace, and did more to explain the concept than any other biblical writer. And yet, Paul had to grow in grace along with others whom Christ has touched and continues to touch. On his first mis-sionary journey, Paul is accompanied by several companions including Barnabas who has been set aside with Paul by the Holy Spirit for special work.[13] In the party is Barnabas's nephew, a young man named John Mark.

The group sails from Cyprus to the province of Pamphylia, Turkey, and travels a few miles inland to a town called Perga. At this point Luke's account includes the terse phrase ". . . John (Mark) left them to return to Jerusalem."[14] In short, John Mark deserted Paul and Barnabas, but the reason is uncertain.

Mark possibly resented the fact that Paul, actually a "rookie" in the Christian ranks, had replaced Barnabas as leader of the missionary enterprise. To this point, Luke had been talking about Barnabas and Saul (that is, Paul). After some exciting incidents on Cyprus, however, which included Paul's bold confrontation with a sorcerer called Elymas,[15] Barnabas seems to take a backseat. Paul didn't scheme or campaign for leadership; it just happened because he was a natural leader, while Barnabas was more the supportive encourager who could be content with following when necessary. Mark, who was very young—probably a teenager—may not have appreciated the way Paul took over from his uncle so he went home in a huff.

Another theory speculates that, due to Mark's youth, he was weary and possibly afraid of making the journey from Perga up to Pisidian, Antioch, a town about one hundred miles away. This meant traveling some of the roughest and most dangerous roads in the known world. In short, Mark may have chickened out or, as Chrysostom, Bishop of Constantinople in the fourth and fifth centuries, speculated, "Perhaps the lad wanted his mother."[16]

A third explanation speculates on racial prejudice. John Mark was a Jew, son of a woman named Mary, whose home was a center of Christian activity in Jerusalem. It was to Mary's house that Peter hurried after an angel freed him from

prison when Herod jailed him for preaching the Gospel.[17]
Those were days of painful transition, as Jews who had become Christians had to get the idea of allowing Gentiles into
the church. Paul and Barnabas had been set aside for the
express purpose of taking the Gospel to Gentile territories.[18]
Mark had been chosen to go along, but he may have been
having second thoughts about preaching to Gentiles. In other
words, the deep-seated prejudice and racism from centuries of
hatred and dislike by Jews for Gentiles may have proved to be
too much.[19]

Whatever the reason, John Mark left the party and put
himself in disgrace. He came home from the mission field
much as Joseph Cooke had done, in disappointment and
failure (*see* chapter 10).

If failure were always final, we would have heard no more
of John Mark, son of an obscure widow named Mary, one of
the members of the Christian church at Jerusalem. He would
have quietly slipped into the woodwork and lived out his days
hiding from the fears that sent him packing for home. Fortunately for John Mark, he had two things going that kept him
from being a failure: 1. he didn't give up; 2. his Uncle Barney
wouldn't give up on him.

The Quitter Becomes Paul's Favorite

When Paul and Barnabas were ready to start a second missionary journey into Asia to check on the churches they had
started on their first trip, John Mark volunteered for service
again! No doubt it took a lot of humility and courage to ask for
a second chance. If we could have listened in, we might have
heard Paul, the rigid perfectionist, telling Barnabas, "No way.
John Mark gave up on us once. We can't take any more risks."

"But the boy is now older, wiser, and tougher," says Barnabas. "I'm sure he can do it."

"I'm not," answers Paul. "He's a deserter and will probably desert us again. There is just too much at stake. I say it's too risky. I've got to have people I can count on in any situation."

"I'm sorry you feel that way, Paul. Maybe it would be better if I took just Mark and visited the brethren on Cyprus, while you take someone else to check the new churches in Asia."

And so Paul and Barnabas agree to disagree. Paul and Silas head for Asia while Barnabas and his nephew sail for Cyprus and into history.[20]

Nothing is known of John Mark for almost twenty years. Some say he founded the Christian church in Alexandria and Egypt, but there is no reliable record, only tradition and legend. Whatever happened, John Mark and his Uncle Barnabas must have made a good team, and this time Mark didn't fold. Barnabas took a chance on someone whose record had "deserter" and "courage suspect" stamped all over it. The result? John Mark went on to write one of the Gospels, which appears under his name in the New Testament.

Even more significant, perhaps, is a line in one of Paul's later letters. Near the end of his life, chained to a Roman prison guard, Paul writes to Timothy and says, ". . . Get Mark and bring him with you, because he is helpful to me in my ministry."[21]

The quitter whom Paul had rejected twenty years before became someone he held in highest esteem. Instead of groveling in guilt and regret for a mistake, John Mark felt godly sorrow and changed his ways. He realized failure isn't final, drew strength from God's grace, and conquered his fears and weakness.

In a sense, John Mark is Everyman. For who has not known fear and failure and disgrace at some time or other? As John Mark struggled with his knots, grace played a quiet but vital role. From his story, we can draw two valuable lessons regard-

ing grace. In this chapter we will see that it is best shared in
community. In chapter 14, we will ponder how and why it is
always available, even when we fail or fall short.

The Connectedness in Community

When John Mark failed that first time and sneaked back
home ashamed and feeling guilty, automatic negative self-talk
was undoubtedly flooding his thoughts:

> *You're a quitter.*
> *You've embarrassed yourself and your uncle . . .*
> *You should be ashamed.*
> *You're a coward, a failure, and a real loser!*

Terms like self-talk and cognitive therapy weren't around
in the first century. We don't know exactly what Mark did,
but whatever happened he was ready to try the missionary
path again the next time Paul and his uncle came through
town. But when he shows enough humility and gumption to
say, "Look, I'm sorry I blew it last time, will you give me
another chance?" he doesn't hear forgiving words like,
"That's okay, Mark. Those things happen."

Instead, Paul firmly turns him down. Why doesn't Paul
show more forgiveness, more of the same grace of God that he
believes in so fervently himself?

We must remember it is relatively early in Paul's ministry.
The iron discipline Paul practiced when he was Saul the
Pharisee still influences him, and in one sense it always will.
His greatest insights and understandings about grace are sev-
eral years away, in letters yet unwritten to groups of believers
in towns like Corinth, Rome, Colossae, and Ephesus.

Fortunately, Mark's uncle graciously steps into the breach
and intercedes. When Paul won't give, Barnabas suggests a

compromise. And that compromise not only saves the day, but a career of service to the Lord. Barnabas is the true hero of this entire tale. His name means "son of encouragement" and encouragement is just what he gives to a lonely, embarrassed, but determined kid who wants a second chance.

Barnabas was the instrument God used to dispense a special portion of grace to John Mark at a critical time in his life. And apparently Barnabas stayed in touch with his nephew down through the years continuing to support and encourage him. In Barnabas, Mark had the benefit of what my psychologist friend Dave Stoop calls "connectedness"—support and non-judgmental love from someone who cares.

From Self-Talk to Connectedness

When Dave Stoop wrote *Self Talk: Key to Personal Growth* in 1982, he firmly believed it was a basic therapeutic tool that could work well with anyone. Since then, he has discovered there is something many people need even more—what he calls "connectedness."

As we talked over lunch in a restaurant near his offices, I asked him to elaborate on his new discovery.

"Connectedness," he told me, "is what you have when other persons care about you and give you encouragement, support, and insight you can't generate alone. In my work with patients at the hospital, I quickly see some are missing the important element of connectedness to other people at a deep level. For many of these people, self-talk is more frustrating than helpful."

"That's interesting. I find positive self-talk very helpful in untying different knots, especially when I stop negative thoughts and think new and positive ones based on Scripture. . . ."

"Yes, but you have connections. You're bonded to your

wife, Jackie, your children, your grandchildren, and Christian friends. You don't live in emotional internal isolation. Being connected to someone actually helps your mind work better— more objectively."

"Your mind works better? How?"

"You can be detached enough to look at things and turn automatic negative thinking into positive self-talk because you can step back from a situation, so to speak, and assess what's really happening. You aren't all wrapped up in yourself."

"What about the person who says, 'All I need is God—He is my connectedness'?"

"It's true that some people can operate this way. And it's also true that God often works with individuals in Scripture, but my own experience and daily work with troubled people has shown me that in many, many cases they need community and connectedness. That's why the Bible has so much to say about community—doing and being for one another."

"You're saying, then, that individualism doesn't really work. . . ."

"I don't think we can make a blanket statement, because there are people who have developed a very personal but individual relationship to God. What I am saying is that so often, without community and connectedness, we can wind up seeing God as a punitive person—as a guilt producer. We see Him as the elusive One we can never quite get hold of. But in the context of community—even with one other significant person—we can experience God as loving and encouraging. We don't have to live under the tyranny of our shoulds."

Dave's insights apply beautifully to the story of John Mark, who undoubtedly did plenty of shoulding himself after his first washout on the mission field. No doubt John

Mark wrestled with the same questions we all ask ourselves from time to time: Yes, we know our sins are forgiven, but why do we still keep fouling up so much? We can't ignore the shoulds that God has given in His Word. Does obeying His shoulds mean living under tyranny? Or is there another way?

FOURTEEN

▪ Grace Means Shoulds Without Tyranny

In 1984, seventy-two of the finest basketball players in the United States reported to coach Bobby Knight for Olympic tryouts. The highly successful coach from the University of Indiana, Knight was asked to take charge of the Olympic basketball hopes and take charge he did. For all of those seventy-two players, the weeks just prior to the 1984 Summer Games were a cross between Green Beret training and the Israelites' march from Egypt to the Promised Land.

When you play for Knight you listen and obey. Indiana fans still remember the time he literally jerked a player out of the game by the shirt after he committed two mistakes in a row. An irascible perfectionist, Knight has never stood for indifference or disobedience by any of his players. As he held tryouts for the 1984 Olympic team, the slightest infraction of his rules sent some of the best basketball talent in the country packing for home, cut from the squad.

Ironically, Knight even scared players that he liked, such as Wayman Tisdale, the hard-working giant from the University of Oklahoma. During the 1984 Summer Games, Tisdale was quoted: "When I get back to Oklahoma, I'm going back there and hug every mean person that I used to think was mean. . . ."[1]

"Mean" as he might have been, Knight's discipline paid off in a Gold Medal for the American team. His players lived by the rules of basketball and the law—Knight's law—which tolerated no back talk, no mistakes, and, God forbid, no breaking of training.

Although Wayman Tisdale might not agree, Bobby Knight and the Apostle Paul have a lot in common. They would agree on the value and joy in athletic competition, the need to be disciplined and to always play to win. Paul's letters often spoke of races, runners, and only one runner getting the prize.[2] He talked about keeping his body under control so he wouldn't come in last.[3] He spoke of pressing toward the goal[4] and chastised one church saying, "You were running a good race. Who cut in on you and kept you from obeying the truth?"[5]

When Paul summarized his entire life, he said: "I have fought the good fight, I have finished the race, I have kept the faith."[6]

Paul was a competitor, all right. His letters are filled with a desire to serve God, give 110 percent, and never give up. How, then, do we account for Romans 7 and all that wretchedness about not being able to do what he wants to do and doing what he knows he shouldn't? Why does Paul feel so wretched? Is he in some kind of spiritual slump? Does he deserve to be benched or even kicked off the team? Paul does not give us specifics, and all we know is that he struggles in the pit of despair. Fortunately, he suddenly realizes that, while athletic analogies have their place, you can put too much emphasis on going for the gold.

It occurs to Paul that his negative self-talk is clouding his thinking. If grace means anything, it guarantees that the Christian's relationship to God is not based on how well he or she performs. God is in the business of developing people, true, but He does not come at it like a coach. By the very nature of his job, the coach has to be ultimately concerned with the bottom line: statistics, improvement, and the win-loss record. When you play for a coach, you live by the rules and your standing is based on your performance. Make mistakes or break training and you pay the price.

But Paul knows he is serving God and playing on His team. His standing on the team is assured because he lives by grace not the law of performance. Paul knows that he is not benched or kicked off the team for poor play. In fact, God doesn't treat him as he might deserve. God graciously sees to it that he not only stays in the game but now he has a chance to win. Now the battle is no longer between Paul's mind and his weak human nature. It is no longer a hopeless conflict between knowing what is right and not being able to do it. Now Paul senses a chance for victory as he realizes he has a new and powerful ally—the Spirit of life in Christ Jesus.[7]

The greatest truth about grace is that it is always available. It doesn't suddenly vanish or become scarce when we fail or fall short. When the tyranny of the shoulds moves in to torture and taunt us, God says: "Hold on, you may tyrannize yourself with your list of shoulds, but I refuse to be a part of those. Yes, I have some very important shoulds that I want you to do, but they are shoulds without tyranny!"

As Paul struggles out of the despair of Romans 7 into the hope and victory of Romans 8, he is learning a crucial lesson: God's shoulds are there to guide, not condemn. Yes, he has failed. Yes, he is weak, but it doesn't matter because God does not limit or ration His love according to our ability to perform or obey laws. Our relationship to God is based not on law but on faith. That's why chapter 8 of Romans opens with good news: There is no condemnation for anyone who has sincerely accepted God's free gift of grace by trusting in Christ.

Salvation—Before and After

One way to picture Paul's struggles is shown in the following diagrams.[8] *Before salvation* there are barriers between God and us (*see* Diagram 1). Those barriers are established on both sides. Although God loves us and yearns for our companionship, there are still barriers on His side because of our sin. By His very nature He is holy and must reject the unholy.[9]

Before Salvation		
Barriers on God's Side		Barriers on Our Side
God		Us

DIAGRAM 1

God's justice (Law) demands punishment for sin.[10] On our side the barriers are also up because of our fear, rebellion, and instinctive awareness of our own guilt and weakness.

After salvation there is a balanced state, which finds the barriers down on both sides (*see* Diagram 2). God now accepts us because His perfect standard (the Law) has been met in Jesus Christ.[11] Now the way is clear for perfect fellowship. Our fear, rebellion, and guilt are gone. The stage is set for God and us to live happily ever after—except for one thing. We still have our old, sinful nature—what the Bible calls "the flesh."

Bible expositor Stuart Briscoe points out that Paul uses the term *flesh* in different ways in the New Testament. But here in Romans 8, he is talking about what is ". . . in contrast to God and His work in human lives, it means human nature with particular reference to its built-in sinfulness . . . the flesh

After Salvation—Balanced		
Barriers on God's Side		Barriers on Our Side
God		Us

DIAGRAM 2

is an attitude or inclination operating in complete rejection of the divine will . . . choosing rather the free expression of anything and everything that will bring self-gratification."[12]

Our flesh is what causes things to get unbalanced. This unbalanced state occurs all too soon. Though saved, we still sin. We still break the rules. We break training, if you please. Back up goes the barrier (*see* Diagram 3). But look carefully. *There is no barrier on God's side.* That barrier was removed forever when we believed in Christ and became new creatures in Him.[13] *The only barrier is on our side.* We erect that barrier when our guilt feelings cause fear and loss of self-esteem, not to mention frustration and dismay. This is the state of mind Paul is describing in Romans 7 when he agonizes because he does what he hates and fails to do what he knows he should.

Fortunately, Paul "comes to himself" and remembers that, no matter how guilt-ridden and frustrated he might feel, God

After Salvation—Unbalanced		
Barriers on God's Side		**Barriers on Our Side**
God		Us

DIAGRAM 3

has no barrier up. That's why Paul practically shouts: "Thanks be to God—through Jesus Christ our Lord! . . . there is now no condemnation for those who are in Christ Jesus. . . ."[14]

Guilt feelings don't destroy your relationship to Christ. The bond between Him and you is unbreakable. *Nothing* can separate you from His love.[15]

When guilt floods in, face it, confess it, repent in godly sorrow, and get on with your life. In many cases, that will take care of how you feel. In other cases, gnawing feelings of inadequacy, hypocrisy, weakness, and even dirtiness will hang around the edges, particularly if you are a perfectionist. Accept those feelings and reclaim the promises in 1 John 1:9: If you confess your sins, God is always just and faithful to forgive your sins and cleanse you from unrighteousness.

Grace is a bottomless mystery. In our puny attempts to fathom it, we can imagine God saying: "What is grace? Grace means that you should obey My law, *but if you don't, I still love you.* You should do My will, *but if you don't, I still love you.* You should try, *but you don't have to succeed to keep My love.* Remember, I don't depend on your ability, resources, or feelings. In fact, my grace works best when you depend entirely on Me."

"But what of our knots, Lord?" we may ask. "We could serve You and do Your will so much better without them."

"Are you sure?" He responds. "Perhaps your knots are what make you lean on Me and without them you would fall into total pride and self-satisfaction. Trust Me. Your knots will be untied in due time."

Do You Try to Get God to Like You Better?

Writing in *Christianity Today*, Philip Yancey poses a knot-related question: "Do I prefer the comfort of a 'childish relationship' with God? Do I cling to legalism as a form of security, and a delusive way of getting God to 'like me better'?"[16]

One thing we must grasp is that, while God does not approve of our actions that cause our knots, He always accepts us. We do not have to jump through legalistic hoops to get God to accept us, because He already accepts us in Christ.

The premise of this book is very simple: We all have knots. We can try to untie them ourselves—and sometimes we succeed quite admirably. But there are always those knots we cannot untie. There are always knots that remind us we must trust in God's grace for all things big and small.

A poem by Annie Johnson Flint catches the power of grace that is great enough to deal with any knot.

> *His grace is great enough to meet the great things,*
> *The crashing waves that overwhelm the soul,*
> *The roaring winds that leave us stunned and breathless,*
> *The sudden storms beyond our life's control.*
>
> *His grace is great enough to meet the small things,*
> *The little pin-prick troubles that annoy,*
> *The insect worries, buzzing and persistent,*
> *The squeaking wheels that grate upon our joy.*[17]

Live the "As Ifs," Not the "What Ifs"

Earlier we looked at two ways to untie our knots: Think ourselves into a new way of acting, and act ourselves into a new way of thinking. Both approaches have their place, and both are deeply affected by our self-talk. Automatic negative thinking can keep us tied in the knot of "what if?" and we will be unable to act at all. Our "what ifs?" spawn worry, anxiety, and fear. Our "what ifs?" feed perfectionism, procrastination, and guilt. But we have another choice. We can live "as if" with faith and trust. It is possible to live as if your knots are untied—as if you have no worries or anxieties, as if you have no fears or hang-ups about doing everything "perfectly."

This isn't Pollyannish thinking; it is simple faith. The writer of the letter to the Hebrews was describing the "as if" approach to life when he said: "Now faith is being sure of what we hope for and certain of what we do not see."[18]

It isn't all done at once. Take baby steps toward trusting more in God and less in your own ability to control things. Take one of your knots and begin to replace your "what if" self-talk with "as if" self-talk that centers on trusting in God's grace, which can untie any knot—if you are willing to let Him.[19]

Are You Weak Enough to Be Strong?

Paul learned that the "as if" approach takes patience—a great deal of patience. In his second letter to the church at Corinth, he speaks of a "thorn in the flesh" sent to torment him. Three times he asks God to take it away, but all God ever tells him is, "My grace is sufficient for you, my power is made perfect in your weakness."[20]

Writing in *Eternity* magazine, J. I. Packer observes that Paul's words on weakness sound foreign in a success-happy society, which admires the tight body, assertive manner, and being cool and in control. Those who take matters into their own hands are heroes and role models; those with personal limitations and handicaps are looked on with deferential pity that often hides a touch of contempt.

Paul himself felt the sting of sneers by the Corinthians who said his ". . . . actual presence is feeble and his speaking beneath contempt."[21] And nothing has changed much. As Packer says, "The world never has time for weakness in any form."[22]

How does being weak make you strong? Packer defines strength as the ability to make an effort. Scripture speaks of

God providing strength to endure the strain and pressures of life, to serve God, and to resist Satan. No one has demonstrated these strengths on earth more ably than Jesus Himself, and He makes them available through His Holy Spirit to all who call Him Savior.

But, says Packer, we must grasp one crucial point. The Spirit only imparts strength when the Christian feels weak, unable to "take matters into his or her own hands." The weakness may be emotional, mental, physical, or spiritual, but in any case it causes the believer to grasp faith in God as a drowning person clutches a life preserver. There is no truer prayer, says Packer, than the sincere cry, "Help!" because ". . . it is weakness at its most explicit and it's a prayer God answers."[23]

Besides never being relieved of his "thorn," Paul went through beatings, shipwreck, and imprisonment. He had more than his share of pain and disappointment and danger. And he adds: "Apart from such external things, there is the daily pressure upon me of concern for all the churches. Who is weak without my being weak? Who is led into sin without my intense concern?"[24]

Paul had his times of worry and fear. He wrestled with guilt feelings as his "all or nothing" sense of commitment kept him battling the depression of perfectionism. But he always had strength to take the pressure, be true to God, and resist Satan. His knots never stopped him because he always reminded himself, ". . . this happened that we might not rely on ourselves but on God. . . ."[25] Paul said he would prefer to be content with weaknesses, insults, distresses, persecutions, difficulties—and knots—for Christ's sake, because when he was weak, then he was strong![26]

God's grace is sufficient for your knots and mine. When those knots seem to grow tighter, we must *STOP* and *THINK*. Then we must ask, "How weak am I? Am I weak enough to be strong?"

In Summary

1. Legalism is no way across the performance gap between God's standards and our weaknesses. "Trying harder" only makes it worse.

2. Cheap grace (lawlessness) is no answer either. Soaking in "hot tub religion" doesn't loosen our knots; it tightens them.

3. To speak of cheap grace is to imply there is costly grace. This costly grace is a way of life that relies totally on God's help and power, not self-effort.

4. The story of John Mark, writer of the Gospel of Mark, illustrates the need to share grace in community. Feeling connected to someone who gives unconditional love and encouragement is the vital element many, if not most, of us need to untie our knots.

5. Although Paul often used athletic analogies to refer to the spiritual life, he emphasizes that the Christian's relationship to God is not based on how well he or she performs.

6. God does not bench us or kick us off His team for poor play or breaking training. He keeps us in the game and empowers us to win.

7. The greatest truth about grace is that it is always available. It doesn't become scarce when we foul up.

8. There are no barriers between us and God, unless we choose to raise them.

9. God does not approve of our knots, but He accepts us.

10. Living the "What if?" life ties us in knots. Living "as if" means trusting more in God and less in our own ability to control things.

11. To be strengthened by God, we must first admit our weaknesses. The truest prayer is simply, "Help!" and it is a prayer God answers.

12. God's grace is sufficient. His power is made perfect in our knots.

■ Source Notes

Chapter 1: You Can Untie Your Knots If . . .

1. Karen Horney, *Neurosis and Human Growth* (New York: W. W. Norton & Company, Inc., 1950), pp. 64, 65.
2. Kathy C. Miller, *Out of Control* (Waco, Tex.: Word Books, 1984), pp. 20, 21.
3. John 5:9 PHILLIPS.
4. William Barclay, *The Gospel of John, Volume 1, The Daily Study Bible* (Edinburgh: The St. Andrew Press, 1955), p. 175.
5. Ibid.
6. "The 80's Are Over," *Newsweek,* January 4, 1988, especially pp. 43, 44.
7. Acts 17:28.

Chapter 2: Does God Help Those Who Help Themselves?

1. Paul Faulkner, *Making Things Right* (Fort Worth: Sweet Publishing, 1986), p. 57.
2. Frank B. Minirth and Paul D. Meier, *Happiness Is a Choice* (Grand Rapids: Baker Book House, 1978), p. 174.
3. Quoted by Paul Faulkner in *Making Things Right,* p. 58.

4. Ibid.
5. Philippians 2:13 NIV.
6. Philippians 2:12 LETTERS.
7. For the full account of Moses' encounter with God at the burning bush *see* Exodus 3:1—4:17.

Chapter 3: Halt! What Worrisome Thought Goes There?

1. Marcus Aurelius, translated by George Long, *The Meditations of Marcus Aurelius* (Garden City, N.Y.: A Dolphin Reprint, Doubleday & Company, Inc., 1873).
2. David Stoop, *Self-Talk: Key to Personal Growth* (Old Tappan, N.J.: Fleming H. Revell Company, 1982), pp. 31ff.
3. 2 Corinthians 10:5 NIV.
4. 1 Peter 1:13 NIV.
5. Stoop, *Self-Talk*, p. 48.
6. Wayne Dyer, *Your Erroneous Zones* (New York: Avon Books, 1977), p. 114.
7. Stoop, *Self-Talk*, p. 94.
8. Dyer, *Your Erroneous Zones*, p. 119.
9. Ibid., p. 121.
10. Ibid.
11. Ernest A. Fitzgerald, *How to Be a Successful Failure* (New York: Atheneum/SMI, 1978), p. 58.

Chapter 4: Stop, Think, and Trust

1. H. Norman Wright, *The Healing of Fears* (Eugene, Ore.: Harvest House Publishers, 1982), pp. 78–84.
2. Quoted in Kevin Leman, *Bonkers* (Old Tappan, N.J.: Fleming H. Revell Company, 1987), pp. 155, 156.
3. Matthew 6:34 NIV.
4. Isaiah 40:27–31 TLB.

5. Ronald Youngblood, *Themes From Isaiah* (Ventura, Calif.: Regal Books, 1984), p. 115.
6. Wright, *The Healing of Fears*, p. 85.

Chapter 5: Nothing to Fear But Failure

1. Denis Waitley, *Being the Best* (Nashville: Oliver-Nelson Books, 1987), p. 134.
2. The original source of this story is unknown. This version is adapted from Dr. Ernest A. Fitzgerald, *How to Be a Successful Failure* (New York: Atheneum/SMI, 1978), pp. 7, 8.
3. Ibid.
4. Gerhard Gschwandtner and Laura B. Gschwandtner, *Super Sellers: Portraits of Success From Personal Selling Power* (Amacom, American Management Association, 1986), p. 8.
5. Ibid., p. 9.
6. Ibid.

Chapter 6: How to Fail Successfully

1. Susan Jeffers, *Feel the Fear and Do It Anyway* (New York: Harcourt Brace Jovanovich Publishers, 1987), pp. 13–16.
2. Ibid., pp. 22–30.
3. Ibid., p. 153.
4. Dr. Ernest A. Fitzgerald, *How to Be a Successful Failure* (New York: Atheneum/SMI, 1978), p. 37.
5. Viktor Frankl, *Man's Search for Meaning* (New York: Pocketbooks, Washington Square Press, 1959, 1984), p. 122.
6. Colossians 3:23.
7. Jill Briscoe, *How to Follow the Shepherd When You're Being Pushed Around by the Sheep* (Old Tappan, N.J.: Fleming H. Revell Company, 1982), pp. 21, 22.
8. 1 John 4:18.
9. Psalms 27:1 NIV.
10. Briscoe, *How to Follow the Shepherd*, p. 29.

Chapter 7: Staying Out From Under the Gun

1. Edwin C. Bliss, *Doing It Now* (New York: Bantam Books, 1984), p. 2.
2. Karl Olsson, *Seven Sins and Seven Virtues* (New York: Harper and Bros., 1959), p. 35.
3. 2 Thessalonians 3:10, 11 NKJV.
4. John 11:1–44.
5. *See* especially John 11:4, 14, 15.
6. Edward R. Dayton and Ted W. Engstrom, *Strategy for Living* (Ventura, Calif.: Regal Books, 1976), p. 66.
7. Charles E. Hummel, "The Tyranny of the Urgent" (Downers Grove, Ill.: Intervarsity Press, 1967).
8. Ibid.

Chapter 8: How to Prioritize Your Priorities

1. Denis Waitley, *Being the Best* (Nashville: Oliver-Nelson Books, 1987), pp. 146, 147.
2. Edward R. Dayton and Ted W. Engstrom, *Strategy for Living* (Ventura, Calif.: Regal Books, 1976), p. 76.
3. Erwin Lutzer, *How to Say No to a Stubborn Habit* (Wheaton, Ill.: Victor Books, 1979), p. 92.
4. Jhan Robbins and Dave Fisher, *How to Make and Break Habits* (New York: Peter H. Wyden, Inc., 1973), pp. 147–149.
5. Matthew 23:1–36.
6. *See* John 12:20–27.
7. Romans 8:38, 39.

Chapter 9: How to Commit Suicide—Perfectly

1. David Stoop, *Living With a Perfectionist* (Nashville: Oliver-Nelson Books, 1987), p. 34.
2. Ibid., pp. 34, 35.

3. Abby Belson, "The Perfection Principle: Are You Too Good for Your Own Good?" *Mademoiselle*, September 1984, p. 310.
4. Kevin Leman, *The Birth Order Book* (Old Tappan, N.J.: Fleming H. Revell Company, 1985), p. 67.

Chapter 10: Pursuing Perfection Versus Seeking Excellence

1. James Dobson, *Emotions: Can You Trust Them?* (Ventura, Calif.: Regal Books, 1980), p. 24.
2. Joseph Cooke, *Free for the Taking* (Old Tappan, N.J.: Fleming H. Revell Company, 1975), p. 9.
3. Grant Howard, *Balancing Life's Demands: A New Perspective on Priorities* (Portland, Ore.: Multnomah Press, 1983), p. 19.
4. Adapted from David Stoop, *Living With a Perfectionist* (Nashville: Oliver-Nelson Books, 1987), p. 59.
5. Ted W. Engstrom, *The Pursuit of Excellence* (Grand Rapids: Zondervan Publishing House, 1982), pp. 32, 33.
6. Ecclesiastes 9:10 NIV.
7. Adapted from Kevin Leman, *The Birth Order Book* (Old Tappan, N.J.: Fleming H. Revell Company, 1985), p. 70.
8. Joseph Cooke, *Free for the Taking*, p. 46.
9. Ibid.
10. Matthew 11:28–30.

Chapter 11: Why Guilt Is the Gordian Knot

1. Karl Menninger, *Whatever Became of Sin?* (New York: Hawthorn Books, 1973), pp. 1, 2.
2. Paula and Dick McDonald, *Guilt-Free* (New York: Ballantine Books, 1978), p. 6.
3. Richard M. Haywood, *Ancient Greece and the Near East* (New York: David McKay Company, Inc., 1964), p. 573.

4. S. Bruce Narramore, *No Condemnation* (Grand Rapids: Zondervan Publishing House, 1984), p. 27.
5. Abby Avin Belson, "Can Guilt Be Good for You?" *Mademoiselle*, October 1981, p. 62.
6. Paul Tournier, *Grace and Guilt* (New York: Harper & Row, 1962), p. 60.
7. *See* Romans 7:15.
8. Romans 7:16–23.
9. Dianne Hales, "You've Done Your Best, Why Do You Still Feel Guilty?" *McCalls*, June 1983.
10. From Helen Block Lewis, *Psychic War in Men and Women*, quoted by Dianne Hales in "You've Done Your Best, Why Do You Still Feel Guilty?" *McCalls*, June 1983.
11. Carol Orsborn, *Enough Is Enough: Exploding the Myth of Having It All* (New York: Putnam, 1986), p. 23ff.
12. Ibid., p. 41.
13. Romans 7:18, 19 NIV.
14. Arthur Bloch, *Murphy's Law, Book III* (Los Angeles: Price/Stern/Sloan Publishers, Inc., 1982), pp. 10, 11.
15. *See* Romans 7:25—8:1.

Chapter 12: Are Guilt Trips Ever Necessary?

1. Fritz Ridenour, *How to Be a Christian Without Being Religious* (Ventura, Calif.: Regal Books, 1967).
2. Ephesians 4:1.
3. *See* Galatians 5:13–18; Romans 8:5–8.
4. Paul Tournier, *Guilt and Grace* (New York: Harper & Row, 1962), p. 48.
5. Dwight L. Carlson, *Guilt Free* (Eugene, Ore.: Harvest House Publishers, 1983), see pp. 42, 43.
6. Archibald Hart, *Feeling Free* (Old Tappan, N.J.: Fleming H. Revell Company, 1979), p. 144.
7. Ibid., p. 147.

8. Bruce Narramore, *No Condemnation* (Grand Rapids: Zondervan Publishing House, 1984), p. 23.

9. Ibid., p. 33.

10. "10-Year-Old Twin Boys Attempt Suicide After Scolding by Father," *Los Angeles Times*, August 27, 1975, Part I, p. 21.

11. For these concepts on "constructive godly sorrow," I am indebted to Bruce Narramore and Bill Counts, *Freedom From Guilt* (Eugene, Ore.: Harvest House Publishers, 1974), pp. 123–127.

12. *See* Matthew 5:48.

13. 2 Peter 3:18 NKJV.

14. "I Was Risking My Job," *Flight Pattern*, Vol. IX, No. 4, December 1984, p. 1.

Chapter 13: The Bridge Over Performance Gap

1. Joseph Cooke, *Free for the Taking* (Old Tappan, N.J.: Fleming H. Revell Company, 1975), p. 16ff.

2. Burt Ghezzi, "Guilt: The Gift That Keeps on Giving," *Eternity*, February 1986, p. 21.

3. *See* Romans 6:1.

4. J. I. Packer, *Hot Tub Religion* (Wheaton, Ill.: Tyndale House Publishers, Inc., 1987), pp. 67, 68.

5. Dietrich Bonhoeffer, *The Cost of Discipleship* (New York: The Macmillan Company, Macmillan Paperback Edition, 1963), p. 47.

6. Ibid.

7. Hebrews 4:16.

8. John 3:16.

9. Romans 3:1–23.

10. Ephesians 2:8, 9.

11. Lawrence O. Richards, *Expository Dictionary of Bible Words* (Grand Rapids: Zondervan Publishing House, 1985), p. 320.

12. Acts 9.

13. Acts 13:1–3.

14. Acts 13:13 NIV.

15. Acts 13:4–12.

16. William Barclay, *The Acts of the Apostles*, *The Daily Study Bible* (Edinburgh: The St. Andrew Press, 1953), p. 108.

17. Acts 12:1–19.

18. Acts 13:1–3.

19. Barclay, *The Acts of the Apostles*, p. 108.

20. Acts 15:36–41.

21. 2 Timothy 4:11 NIV.

Chapter 14: Grace Means Shoulds Without Tyranny

1. Mark Heisler, "Knight: In Pursuit of Perfection," *Los Angeles Times*, Day 12 Coverage of Olympics '84, Wednesday, August 8, 1984, p. 18.

2. 1 Corinthians 9:24.

3. 1 Corinthians 9:27.

4. Philippians 3:14.

5. Galatians 5:7 NIV.

6. 2 Timothy 4:7 NIV.

7. Romans 8:1–5.

8. For these "before and after salvation" diagrams, I am grateful to Bruce Narramore and Bill Counts, *Freedom From Guilt* (Eugene, Ore.: Harvest House Publishers, 1974), pp. 83–85. Used by permission.

9. Ezekiel 39:7; Habakkuk 1:13.

10. Romans 1:8; 2 Thessalonians 1:8, 9; Hebrews 9:22.

11. Romans 3:21–24.

12. Stuart Briscoe, *The Communicators' Commentary*, *Romans* (Waco, Tex.: Word Books, 1987), p. 153.

13. 2 Corinthians 5:17.

14. Romans 7:25—8:1 NIV.

15. Romans 8:38, 39.

16. Philip Yancey, "Submitting to Freedom," *Christianity Today*, June 12, 1987, p. 64.

17. Annie Johnson Flint, "Great Grace," p. 120, used by permission of Evangelical Publishers, a division of Scripture Press Publications Limited.

18. Hebrews 11:1 NIV.

19. For the comparison of "what if?" living with "as if" living, I am indebted to Dave Stoop, *Self-Talk: The Key to Personal Growth*, p. 105.

20. *See* 2 Corinthians 12:9.

21. 2 Corinthians 10:10 PHILLIPS.

22. J. I. Packer, "The Way of the Weak Is the Only Healthy Way," *Eternity* magazine, November 1987, p. 28.

23. Ibid.

24. 2 Corinthians 11:28, 29 NAS.

25. *See* 2 Corinthians 1:9.

26. 2 Corinthians 12:10.